Ideas for Writing

CREATIVE CHRISTMAS LETTERS

That People Are Actually Eager to Read!

Janet Colbrunn

Website: www.writingcreativechristmasletters.com

Library of Congress Control Number: 2006910239

ISBN-13: 978-0-9790708-0-8

ISBN -10: 0-9790708-0-5

First edition published by Baycourt Publishing, 2007

Design and layout by Kaylin Davis, KayMac Designs

Manufactured in the United States of America

*Dedicated to my family members who have provided me
with both stimulation and inspiration for writing
creative Christmas letters year after year.*

*Special appreciation goes to my children and their
spouses who have been eager to carry on
the letter-writing tradition in their
own families and have graciously
provided their own unique letters
for use in this publication.*

Table of Contents

Creative Christmas Letters
Introduction

Christmas has long been a time of joyfully gathering with family and friends to celebrate the birth of Christ but is especially exhilarating when we can share it with those who do not live close enough to visit frequently. Relationships are renewed by sharing events of the past year and plans for the year to come in a warm environment filled with food and fun. In addition to the parties and gatherings, Christmas has been a time to send greetings and best wishes in the form of cards. Although the first ones were quite expensive and were sent mainly by the elite in the early to mid 1800's, affordable ones were available by the 1850's. Boxed cards were not readily available and popular until the 20th century and the 100-year-old tradition continues today with 70% of Americans sending 2.5 billion holiday cards each year.

The nearly 2000 greeting card publishers in the U.S. today are now competing with more recent forms of holiday greetings. The ease of computer-mediated communication is getting people back into the habit of correspondence by writing and indeed, some are sending holiday greetings by e-mail or developing their own computer-generated cards. However, most consider electronic greetings inappropriate for occasions such as weddings, sympathy or Christmas. Paper greeting cards show that one took the time to consider, and purchase a card just for them. Increasing in popularity are Christmas letters, enhanced with pictures on holiday stationery. Even though duplicated, these letters add a personal touch to our traditional Christmas greeting. Letters are often enclosed within a traditional Christmas card. Just like the holiday gatherings, the Christmas letter helps us to maintain relationships that otherwise risk being lost due to distance and time.

Before Christmas letters became popular among my circle of friends, I was concerned about being accused of writing brag letters. Therefore, I continued to send the traditional cards, laboriously handwriting notes to that ever-increasing number of friends, who moved out of our lives geographically. Encouraged by my husband to be more efficient and effective in our Christmas communication, I was determined to move beyond the simple reporting of facts in a copied letter. Just as anticipation and fun are the heart of holiday gatherings, I decided that our Christmas letters had to be creative and FUN! I wanted people who received them to be eager to open and read them. Oh, that they might pray to never be taken off of our Christmas card list! I knew that I would need help to do something unique every year and notified my husband and three children that they were recruited.

Thus, in 1985, we wrote the first creative Christmas letter from the Colbrunns. Much to my surprise, two other benefits emerged. Every year, during our annual Thanksgiving trip to Grandma's house in Ohio, we held a brainstorming session. We made a list of important topics in each of our lives that would be included, selected a theme, and had great fun thinking of humorous ways to convey our message. As the years went by, we realized that it had become a family bonding tradition and that we were creating a family history log. We have referred back to that log to verify dates many times. Eventually, my daughter gave everyone in the family a notebook, which included all of our Christmas letters to that date. Today, these notebooks also include their own creative Christmas letters, now that they are all married with families of their own.

The annual letter is also a time to share again the true meaning of Christmas and the significance of the birth of Jesus Christ as our Savior. This personal reference bears a stronger message than sending a printed religious Christmas card. It becomes a subtle way of saying to our pre-Christian friends that Jesus is Lord of our lives and that eternal life is only a decision away. It reminds even our Christian friends that we haven't forgotten that Jesus is the reason for the season.

I have compiled this series of creative Christmas letters, written by our family, to be a guide for those who wish to add creativity and humor to their own Christmas greetings. The work is still before the family-author to outline the information to be presented and then to incorporate it into a creative and appealing format. I have included a model of how a list of events can be transformed into a normal letter or woven into a theme to create a letter that is just as informational but more fun to read. The challenge for most is to develop a theme each year and then surprise your readers with a letter that will outdo the last. The themes are divided into three categories: List Letters, Format Letters and Perspective Letters.

List letters can include the "top ten" anything, including books, TV shows, blessings and lessons learned. Surprisingly, one can provide as much family information under the guise of a list of election results or sports statistics as an outright good news/bad news list. Having children can provide an abundance of topics to list. Whether quoting their comments and questions or recording their antics and progress, all can be done in a manner that subtly reports the family news for the year.

Format letters can draw from anything that goes into print. We've used a diary, music lyrics, a Bible verse, letters to Santa, a play-on-words traditional newsletter, newspaper, dictionary, game, yearbook, crossword puzzle and magazine.

In the perspective letters category, we have had letters from the perspective of what the house, the dog, my two-year old grandchild, and our guardian angel might have written about our family. We have also written one from the perspective of having lived 100 years ago including a family picture of how we might have looked.

Part I
Creating Your Letter

Perhaps, you have never written even a traditional Christmas letter. Where do you begin? The first step is to develop a list of topics that could be included in the letter. A fun way to develop these topics is to make it a tradition to hold a letter writing event. Thanksgiving weekend is a good time to create a family slumber party atmosphere in front of a fire with marshmallows or popcorn. Whatever environment that appeals to your family's sense of fun and relaxation would be best. If the teenagers are resistant or too busy for such a family gathering, you may have to capture their attention in the car where they are compelled to be at least physically present. Asking questions such as the following can generate topics: What have we done this year? Where have we gone? What have we accomplished? What changes have occurred? What memories are worth sharing? What occurred that was inspirational or humorous? What are our future plans? Depending on the ages of your children, you may be able to have them generate an individual list of events, accomplishments, and activities and then share them one at a time with the rest of the family. Children of all ages benefit from an activity that celebrates their strengths and values their worth.

Once the topics are identified, the next task is to select a theme for the format. Selecting a theme that distinguishes your letter from a traditional Christmas letter may be even more challenging than blending the data into a thematic format. If you are especially creative, a theme may be one of those back-of-the-mind ideas that just pops up one day. A more logical thinker may be able to study the list of topics and see a theme that really describes that year such as change or a preponderance of good news and bad news. Then there may be a year when nothing new comes to mind. Indeed, I settled for a conventional letter on Christmas stationery one year when under pressure to furnish and decorate our new Florida condo before going home for Christmas. A friend mentioned how she missed getting a fun letter, and that subconsciously set my mind to work. Noticing that our list of topics pertained to new houses and jobs, I realized that I could have done a Classified Ads theme.

The next step is to weave your topic list into the theme you have selected. Sometimes it requires writing a paragraph for each person. Younger children could dictate verbally what can be shared about their lives, while older children could accomplish this task independently. This exercise becomes a practical lesson in creative writing, grammar and spelling. (Indeed, teachers can use creative Christmas letter-writing as an assignment with these goals in mind.) In this stage, the family can brainstorm ideas to add humor and continuity that better fit the theme format. Letters that consist of lists might require one person to do a rough draft of the total letter and allow the others to enhance it. Even when the children have grown and left home, long time friends are still interested in hearing about their lives. In this case, the parents may write the letters but send them to the adult children to critique. It is always best to have at least one other person edit the final draft as a last step. If need be, a friend with writing skills may be willing to be your editor.

Once the text is completed, decisions need to be made concerning the graphics or photos that you want to have included. Some themes are best done on plain white paper. (See Guardian Angel Report on page 81.) Christmas stationery makes an attractive background and often complements your theme as well. Once hard to find, there are a variety of places where holiday stationery can be purchased today. For example, stationery by Geographics can be found at Staples and Walgreens. Office Depot carries Foray brand and Walmart distributes American Pad and Paper holiday stationery. Religious themes are available at Christian bookstores carrying DaySpring products. Be sure to shop early while the selection is still abundant. For more personalized letters, most word-processing programs allow you to insert digital photos or graphics into your letter text. Non-digital photos or your children's artwork can be scanned into a file for use in your document as well. If a letter just doesn't seem to fit the paper, adjusting margins, changing the size or style of font, or using the back or larger sized paper may create the appropriate space.

The last step is to duplicate your letter for distribution. If you want to personalize each greeting or have a small number of copies to make, using your computer printer may give you the best print-out. Otherwise, your local copy shop can copy onto your Christmas stationery directly from your plain white "master." A better idea is to burn your letter onto a CD, photos and all, for the copy shop to reproduce for you if they offer this service. The copies, especially the photos, should be much crisper. Keeping in mind that a color copy is likely to be much more expensive than black and white, you can convert a color photo into "grayscale" to get a nice black and white photo in your letter. In conclusion, stamping and scrapbooking materials may be used to enhance each copy.

An Example of How a Letter Is Developed

The process for writing a traditional or creative letter begins and ends the same. We begin with a list of topics and end with a draft that is enhanced and edited. The difference lies in selecting and utilizing a theme to share your message instead of straight reporting of information. These next three pages demonstrate how both a traditional and a creative letter were drawn out of the same list of topics. Compare the readability of both. Notice that in making a letter more creative, some topics may have to be left out. For some frazzled Christmas season readers, that may be a good thing.

STEP 1. GENERATE A LIST OF TOPICS TO BE INCLUDED IN YOUR LETTER.

FAMILY MEMBERS, FRIENDS OR PETS	EVENTS, TRAVELS, HUMOROUS SITUATIONS, CHANGES, ACCOMPLISHMENTS, ACTIVITIES
Donn & Janet	Buying a condo in Florida
	Helping friends in Arizona
	Sailing trip to BVI with friends
	Helping friend with modular home
	Spending quality time with grandchildren
	Completing the garage foundation project
Christy & Chris	New home
	New jobs
	Puppy
Robb & Joni	New baby due
	Playscape
	Home projects
Jonn & Jen	New home
	Home projects

STEP 2. SELECT A THEME.

In the example on the next page, a "classified ads" theme was selected because new homes and jobs were predominate features in the above list.

STEP 3. WEAVE TOPICS INTO THE THEME.

I chose two classified ad categories that fit the topics:

FOR SALE	HELP WANTED
Condo	Arizona cabin
Nebraska house	Sailing trip
Michigan house	Modular home
	Foundation project
	Home projects

2003 Colbrunn Classified Ads

FOR SALE

Condominium in Venice, Florida. 2 bedrooms and a den in upstairs unit. Just 4 miles from the gulf coast beaches.

We jumped on this one since it was only 15 minutes from the winter home of sister and brother-in- law, Pat and Phil. Plans are to be six-month snowbirds and enjoy the winter months in the sun. Half the fun was shopping and decorating before the winter season.

House on one of the many hills in LaVista, Nebraska, with 4 bedrooms. Good resale potential; perfect for the Air Force family who plans to stay only 3 years. Nearly new and requires some creative landscaping.

Christy, Chris and Ruben, a Wheaton Terrier puppy, moved into this one in July. It is located 15 minutes from the base hospital where Chris is a physician in the clinic, and from Christy's job at a child welfare agency in Omaha.

Four bedroom house in Warren, Michigan, perfect for a family with 2-year old triplets, including a carpeted basement for playtime adjoining a half-walled nook for Mom to pursue her interests.

Jonn and Jen, in desperate need for more living space, found this dream house in September just down the road 15 minutes from their old house. Nevertheless, the additional space just makes the triplets harder to corral for the next activity.

HELP WANTED

Experienced carpenter and designer needed for addition on a mountain cabin in AZ. Contact owners who are eager to escape hot Phoenix summers.

We just couldn't pass up a free working vacation in June with our friends, the Goodwins.

Devoted parents, who are willing to work for food, needed to help put up window treatments, build walls, workbenches, and kiddy playscapes, and do miscellaneous repairs. Bonus includes playing with 5 wonderful grandchildren, plus 1 due in May.

Grandchildren and free food will grab us every time.

Ditch-digger wanted to repair a foundation problem in the corner of garage.

Nobody answered this ad, so Donn ended up spending the month of September single-handedly digging 8 cubic yards by hand, putting in a cement footer and filling in the rest.

Captain and First Mate needed for a 1-week charter on a catamaran in the British Virgin Islands. Snorkeling skills essential. Must be willing to enjoy island cuisine with the Poncars, Geamans, and the Holmans.

After all that work, we signed on for a great time renewing relationships with old friends.

Christians needed to share the good news: that because Jesus was born on Christmas and rose again on Easter, accepting Him, offers us eternal life.

May the Good News of Christmas live in your hearts this Christmas Season!

Compare this traditional letter format to the theme-generated letter on the opposite page.

Colbrunn Christmas 2003

Nearly 20 years ago, you may have received our first official Christmas letter from the "walls" of our new Michigan house. Our first full year of retirement has again been the "year of the house." In fulfillment of our dream to spend future winters in Florida, we spent the month of February searching for the right condo in the right community on the Gulf coast of Florida. We found a two-bedroom and den unit just 4 miles from the beaches in Venice and 15 minutes from the winter home of sister and brother-in-law, Pat and Phil. We plan to spend a month in the fall and 4 months in the winter. If you are planning a trip there, be sure to contact us at 555-382-5680 or djcolbrunn@aol.com. We made return trips for a closing, to take delivery on furniture and to do some decorating. Meanwhile, we spent some time in the spring helping a friend, who needed a home, to purchase and fix up a modular home. Just getting into the trading spaces mode, we had the opportunity to visit Bill and Kathy Goodwin in Arizona for a week where we had fun helping them with an addition onto their cabin in Flagstaff.

With our recent purchasing experience, Chris and Christy asked us to drive to Omaha, Nebraska, location of their next 3-year stint with the Air Force, where we supported Christy in her search for a home there. Since Chris was unable to take more vacation time, she communicated with him by cell phone and digital e-mail photos. They closed a deal on a nearly new house on one of the many hilly areas of Omaha — a big surprise for those of us who expected flat cornfields. Chris is in family practice at the clinic on base and Christy got a job with a child welfare agency. The first thing they did after moving in July, was to get Ruben, a Wheaten Terrier puppy. We returned in November to help Chris build a garage workbench and Christy complete some window treatments.

In the midst of it all, we chartered a catamaran in the British Virgin Islands with three other couples. The sailing was a pleasure with the stability of two hulls, even in heavy winds. We enjoyed the snorkeling, island cuisine and great company of the Poncars, Geamans and Holmans.

Robb and Joni keep expanding their household. We spent some time helping as they built an extensive playscape for the kids and restoring after a major waterproofing job they had done in the basement. The most exciting expansion is the development of Baby #3 due in June. Used to difficult pregnancies, Joni is doing comparatively well this time with the help of some herbs. We're believers! The most enjoyable part of our visits is watching Boyd and Lilia entertain us with their precocious antics.

Donn spent the month of September repairing a major foundation problem in the corner of our garage, digging out eight cubic yards of soil by hand to reinforce the footer with cement. No sooner done, than Jonn and Jen decided that it was time to get a bigger house in Warren. We were off and running again helping to get the old house ready for sale and make adjustments at the new house for triplet 2-year-olds. They now have much more living and bedroom space with a carpeted basement for playtime, complete with a half-walled nook for Jen to pursue her interests. The triplets are still a handful to corral for the next activity, but now that they can talk and interact, it is fun to watch them rapidly discover their world and display their unique personalities.

Whew! It's been a busy year, but next year we promise to play more. On the other hand, we don't get lonely or bored helping on those never-ending home improvement projects. What? You have a job for us? Give us a call; we work for food!

From our house to your house, have a blessed Christmas season, rejoicing in the promise of a heavenly home by simply accepting Jesus as Lord.

PART II
List Letters

List letters are a good choice for beginning a creative Christmas letter tradition. They are easiest to create and simplest to carry through. One could begin by simply doing a family report by the month or by the season. Theme variations can be combined with a chronological listing to enhance the appeal and interest level of the reader. Examples of such variations can be found on the following pages.

In This Section:

Good News/Bad News

Top Ten TV Shows

Top Ten Reasons

Election Results

Year of Firsts

Kid Quotes

Why Questions

Lessons Learned

Blessings

Family Statistics

Sport Statistics

Best Sellers

Good News/Bad News

There are years that seem to be filled with hardship. Those are the years that we grow the most. What a Christmas witness it is, to be able to share the good news that God can create from the bad news! Just the process of writing this letter was healing. This was the perfect letter to include a tract type excerpt called *Why Celebrate Christmas?* I put that on the back of the letter and folded it so that the excerpt was the first thing people saw when they removed the letter from the envelope.

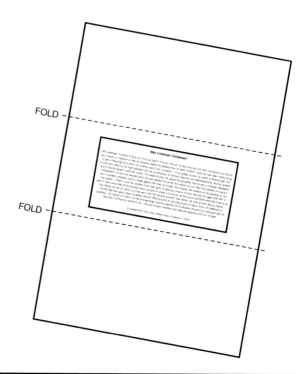

Why Celebrate Christmas?

Why celebrate Christmas if Jesus isn't the true Savior? If he isn't the Son of God, then the only other conclusions are that He was a phony, a madman or that His disciples started the greatest hoax on earth. PHONY? Could He have been merely trying to gain a following? If He were, He certainly wasn't very successful — if you gauge success by power or financial gain. He turned many away by His high standards and His unwillingness to overlook hypocrisy and half-heartedness. And He certainly wasn't tricking people to get their money. The evidence does not support the possibility that He was a charlatan. MADMAN? Self-deceived? Sincere but deluded about His own identity? His words and actions do not reflect the behavior of a person who is mentally unstable. Such a charge against Him does not explain the miracles, the brilliance of His teaching nor His resurrection... HOAX? Could the disciples have been guilty of painting a picture of Jesus that was far bigger than life? It doesn't make sense that all the disciples would conspire to create a monstrous lie that would contradict what they knew to be true. Would you die for what you knew was a lie? The disciples wouldn't have either, yet most of them died as martyrs. TRUTH? We have good reason to believe that the Bible presents an accurate picture of Jesus Christ. His fulfillment of prophecy, His impact on history, His life and teachings, and the response of His disciples all point to a conclusion that He was and is all that He claimed to be — the Son of God. Therefore how shall we respond to the Son of God?

Excerpted from, Why Does It Make Sense to Believe in Christ? RBC

THE BAD NEWS IS...
Some think that Jesus was a phony, a madman or part of a great hoax.

THE GOOD NEWS IS...
He claimed to be the Son of God and invites us to accept Him.

The Bad News Is...

The Good News Is...

The Bad News Is...	The Good News Is...
1998 has been a trying year for the Colbrunns.	1998 has been a year of miracles for the Colbrunns.
The chelation therapy didn't work for Janet because two arteries were 100% blocked.	Bypass surgery was performed in June to allow for more bloodflow.
She had a heart attack during surgery and required a heart pump to recover.	A doctor called her the miracle girl and she made a speedy recovery.
Five weeks later, it was determined that the new bypasses were totally clogged because her receiving arteries were too small to allow the blood to flow at normal speed.	Five months later, the heart disease is reversing and she is feeling better due to a miraculous flow of blood in the previously 100% blocked artery, combined with diet, exercise and more chelation.
Janet's sister, Patty, also had a heart attack and bypass surgery this past spring. It's about those family genes!	Her sisters and hubbies visited them in Michigan to attend the world's largest 50's car show – the Woodward Dream Cruise in August.
Donn didn't have time to work on the Corvette this year – again.	He spent a lot of time learning how to cook, clean and care for his favorite heart patient.
Grandpa Tom at age 87, passed away in February.	He left us with many happy memories of him.
Christy decided to drop out of Hope College for the spring semester and spend time in Colorado Springs, Colorado, instead.	There, she attended Focus on the Family Institute and with 39 other students from across the country, she socialized, studied and got to meet Dr. Dobson.
The phone bills were still high this summer	Christy stayed in Colorado to work as a nanny.
Tuition bills will not end with Christy's graduation from Hope in May since she plans to attend graduate school in the fall.	She learned so much at the Institute about family life and the Christian worldview, that she made a decision to become a Christian counselor.
Robb quit his job and is involved in doing homework again including cutting up cadavers.	He's earning a masters degree in robotics engineering from Case Western Reserve University.
Robb and Joni moved to Parma, Ohio, far away from Clarkston, Michigan.	Now they live 20 minutes from Grandma and just two hours from Joni's parents.
Joni had to quit her job in Michigan.	She landed a job with NASA, her long-time dream.
Jonn and Jen have been working 25 hours a day at their jobs, doing homework and classwork.	They will both be done with graduate school before the next century.
They also spent time battling gusting winds, heavy rains, poison ivy, falling trees, wild vines and buried boulders, armed with borrowed tools.	By the time Jonn and Jen were finished, they had converted their overgrown backyard jungle into a nicely landscaped lawn.
Daisy, in a frenzy over a neighborhood dog, jumped (or fell) off of our 10 foot high deck.	She came running back home and acted like nothing unusual happened. Another miracle!
Our household has not yet been deemed to be Y2K compliant.	We still have one more year to prepare for the worst and hope for the best.

Top Ten TV Shows

Depending on how much television you watch, writing a Top Ten TV Shows list will be a cinch or a challenge. I ended up using some oldies because I wasn't familiar enough with the current listings. One has to be careful about using dated material. After reading the names of the sponsors for the TV shows, my daughter asked what Geritol was.

STEP 1. GENERATE YOUR OWN LIST OF TOPICS TO BE INCLUDED IN YOUR LETTER.

FAMILY MEMBERS, FRIENDS OR PETS	EVENTS, TRAVELS, HUMOROUS SITUATIONS, CHANGES, ACCOMPLISHMENTS, ACTIVITIES

STEP 2. YOUR THEME IS "TOP TEN TV SHOWS."

STEP 3. WEAVE TOPICS INTO THE THEME.
Brainstorm some shows that might be used.

COLBRUNN'S TOP TEN TV SHOWS FOR 2000

10. THE SURVIVOR   Sponsored by Geritol
Working hard to be the last guy left... at the office, Donn goes to work early and comes home late with his lap top in tow to do more work at home. Nevertheless, he makes time to direct finance committee meetings at church and work on home-improvement projects for his wife and kids. Don't nobody tell him that there ain't a million dollars waiting for the guy who survives this pace for 3 more years — just retirement! His e-mail address is jdcolbrunn@aol.com if you know how to add hours onto a day.

9. HAPPY DAYS   Sponsored by AAA
In contrast to Donn's hectic pace, Janet enjoys working part-time and takes on volunteer activities to ease into retirement gradually. She uses phony excuses to lure Donn away from work like: 1) Let's go see the Annapolis Boat Show (and spend the weekend with Christy). 2) Let's go for a boat ride with the Wagners (and take a Western Carribean Cruise). 3) Let's use our frequent flyer tickets on your next business trip (and take Grandma and Christy to see the Grand Canyon). 4) Let's do dinner and a play with the Piataks and Luhs (at Niagara-on-the-Lake and take in the falls at night). 5) Let's get rid of that avocado bathtub (and get an air jet tub).

8. WHEELS OF FORTUNE   Sponsored by Firestone Tires
The grand prize 1961 Corvette was declined by the winning contestant because it would take more time and money to restore than it was worth. Maybe next year!

7. HOME IMPROVEMENT   Sponsored by Home Depot
What started out as "getting a new dishwasher" for Jonn and Jen ended up as a totally remodeled kitchen. The job looked so easy (and cost so much) that they decided to try building a new deck on their own. It turned out great and Jen gained the reputation for being the fastest cordless driller in the Midwest.

6. TOUCHED BY AN ANGEL   Sponsored by Toys Really R Us
Somewhere in his first year of life, an angel told Boyd that eating and sleeping is not as much fun as walking, talking and exploring the world of toys. He also learned that if you are good when Grandpa and Grandma baby-sit, they will buy you lots more toys. In addition, he discovered how to reprogram the telephone message machine with "Da da, da da, da da, beep."

5. MOVIE OF THE WEEK: WEDDING SINGERS   Sponsored by Sound Studios, Inc.
Robb and Joni cannot go to a wedding without being invited to sing a Toast-to-the-Bride-and-Groom song at the reception. Be sure to book them early for your next family wedding. They are busy playing in the praise band at church and remodeling (including a 3-room sound studio in the basement) their new house in Hinckley, Ohio.

4. WORLD BUSINESS REVIEW   Sponsored by Butterfly Ballots, Inc.
Creative Memories stock keeps rising thanks to Jen and Joni Colbrunn. Robb Colbrunn brings us a late-breaking report from the Cleveland, Ohio, area showing that the final vote counts have just been certified in favor of Codonics over NASA. Robb recently inaugurated his work with Codonics, manufacturer of medical printers. Meanwhile, in Dearborn, Michigan, Jonn Colbrunn reports no opposition to his promotion to performance consulting supervisor at MSX International. Let the chads fall as they may!

3. WHO WANTS TO BE A MILLIONAIRE   Sponsored by Eden Counseling Service
With no lifelines left, Christy had to choose the hardest part about being a counseling intern: 1) Finding time to do homework for 2 classes. 2) Having clients with procrastination issues who don't show-up. 3) Having an office in the staff kitchen. 4) Receiving 3 suicide calls in 2 days on the off-hours beeper. Unable to make a decision, she relinquished her winnings to go home to finish a paper and study for an exam. She plans to graduate from Regent University in May.

2. 7TH HEAVEN   Sponsored by Cloud 9 Bathroom Tissue
Christy's been in 7th heaven since she met Chris Tanner in Virginia Beach. However, they have had to maintain a long distance relationship since he moved to Washington D.C. He's a captain in the Air Force, doing his residency at the Andrews Air Force Base Hospital.

1. AMERICA'S MOST NEEDED   Sponsored by God
If America ever needed to be rescued from a downhill moral slide, it is now. If America ever needed leaders with decency and integrity, it is now. If America ever needed a guide and a savior, it is now. If America ever needed to personally know the Christ of Christmas, it is now. May you experience His joy and peace on this 2000th anniversary of His birth!

Top Ten Reasons

The Top Ten Reasons to Visit Nebraska, was written by my daughter and her husband the year that they made a big move. This is an ideal theme to use when one moves to a new location. Details about your new life can be readily woven into this format while notifying friends of your new address. Be sure to send this letter out early so that everyone will use the right address.

STEP 1. GENERATE YOUR OWN LIST OF TOPICS TO BE INCLUDED IN YOUR LETTER.

FAMILY MEMBERS, FRIENDS OR PETS	EVENTS, TRAVELS, HUMOROUS SITUATIONS, CHANGES, ACCOMPLISHMENTS, ACTIVITIES

STEP 2. YOUR THEME IS "TOP TEN REASONS."

STEP 3. WEAVE TOPICS INTO THE THEME.
Identify some potential reasons.

Merry Christmas & Happy New Year!
Top 10 Reasons to Visit Nebraska

10. The Tanners live there now. Thanks to the Air Force, Chris' job was relocated to Offutt Air Force base in Omaha. It came as quite a surprise, as their top 20 choices of where to move mainly consisted of European and East Coast bases. When told none of those were available and the choices now included places such as Turkey, Guam, North Dakota or Louisiana, Nebraska appeared to be a blessing. Welcome to the Heartland!

9. Stay in Chris and Christy's new home. Tired of renting, they were able to purchase their first house in La Vista, just south of Omaha. The house was six months old when they moved in, so they have spent many weekends working on decorating and landscaping. They have plenty of space and welcome visitors.

8. Meet Ruben, the dog. After one week in their new home, the dog-loving couple finally got their pooch! Ruben is now an eight-month-old Wheaten Terrier. He is a shaggy-looking medium size dog with a fun fur-sonality!

7. Get medical advice from a "real" doctor. As Christy jokes with Chris, he is official now that he finished his residency program and passed his medical board exam. He is putting all that knowledge to use in a family health clinic at the hospital on base. His hours are better than residency, but his empanelment of 2,000 patients makes for busy and long days.

6. See Christy in CSI. No, she isn't on the TV show, but she is working at the Child Saving Institute. After a few months of job hunting, she found a position as a therapist and intake coordinator. She works with the public schools to help children and their families get connected to the resources they need. She was sad to leave her previous job at Bethany Christian Services, but hopes to somehow continue supporting the mission of adoption.

5. Fly easily to the Midwest. The Tanners have concluded that one of the best parts of Omaha is the convenient airport. This makes getting away from the middle of America easy, as they enjoyed a cruise in the Caribbean this fall. The airport also allows family and friends to visit, as some have already done.

4. Experience Cornhusker mania. While learning their new culture, Chris and Christy have discovered just how devoted fans are to the University of Nebraska football team. The stadium becomes the 3rd largest city in the state on game day and it would be a major faux pas to wear anything but red, the school color. To add to their enjoyment of Midwest culture, they have visited enough fairs, corn mazes and farming expos to last a lifetime!

3. Witness Christy bowling. Much to her dismay, Chris signed them up for a neighborhood bowling league. They enjoy the monthly event to get to know their neighbors and develop a sense of community. In addition, they have joined a church Bible study and become active in a local Young Life committee. Chris has been brushing up his soccer skills while participating in a work league and Christy is gaining a better understanding of being a military wife through involvement in a medical spouses group.

2. Taste the official state soft drink. A pitcher of Kool-Aid awaits your visit! Kool-Aid was named the official soft drink, being developed in Hastings, Nebraska in 1927. In addition, Nebraska offers a state fossil (mammoth), official dance (square dance), home of the world's second richest man (Warren Buffett), automotive replica of Stonehenge (Carhenge), and produces fabulous meat (Omaha Steaks and Spam).

1. The Message of Christmas is just as true in Nebraska as around the world. God sent his only son, Jesus, to be born in a lowly manger and live among us. This act of grace is a gift to all that claim Him as their Savior. Chris and Christy hope that the peace and joy of Christmas are celebrated in your life this season!

Election Results

An intense presidential election year can bring to mind other choices that we make throughout the year. These can range from the trivial to some very personal issues presented in a way that invites prayers and praises.

STEP 1. GENERATE YOUR OWN LIST OF TOPICS TO BE INCLUDED IN YOUR LETTER.

FAMILY MEMBERS, FRIENDS OR PETS	EVENTS, TRAVELS, HUMOROUS SITUATIONS, CHANGES, ACCOMPLISHMENTS, ACTIVITIES

STEP 2. YOUR THEME IS "ELECTIONS RESULTS."

STEP 3. WEAVE TOPICS INTO THE THEME.

What "(fill in the blank) vs. (fill in the blank)" contests can you devise?

2004 Tanner Election Results

During the long election season of 2004, so much attention was focused on the presidential race and other hotly contested issues that you might have missed out on the election debates in the Tanner family this year:

Gambling vs. Vegas Shows

Chris attended a sports medicine conference this past spring in Las Vegas, so Christy decided it was a great opportunity to join in the fun, touring all the hotels and shopping! As hard as the casinos campaigned, only $2 worth of nickels was gambled!

High School vs. College

The Tanners are committee members of Young Life, a Christian ministry to high school students. However, Chris' dream job is to work with college athletes as a sports medicine doctor. He is hoping to pursue further training when he leaves the military in June 2006. The vote is still being tallied on this issue.

Store-bought vs. Homemade

In May, Chris and Christy took a two-week vacation to Italy. They saw the Pope, took a cooking class in Tuscany, rode a gondola in Venice, hiked the coast of the Cinque Terre, and climbed the Leaning Tower of Pisa. Along the way, they were able to fully appreciate Italian food, stuffing themselves on delicious pasta. This election was easily won by homemade pasta!

Terrorism vs. Democracy

Two weeks after the Tanner's Italy vacation, Chris was unexpectedly deployed to Tallil Air Base in southern Iraq for three months. He was restricted to a one square mile base in 130° heat. He worked inside a five-tent hospital as an emergency room doctor. His 24 hours on, 72 hours off shifts left him plenty of time to learn to play the guitar, lead a men's Bible study, play sand volleyball, and win ping-pong and Frisbee golf tournaments. He said it felt like going to a summer camp and had it not been for missing Christy, he would have stayed longer! Creating democracy will get his vote.

Home Alone vs. Traveling the Country

With Chris deployed, Christy decided the best way to cope was to travel the summer away, visiting family and friends around the country. She loved getting to spend time with all their nephews and nieces, reconnect with old friends and most of all, never have to clean a house! Ruben probably had the hardest summer out of the family, as he did not like being shuffled back and forth between strange houses and having to share with other pets! Nevertheless, Christy campaigns heavily in favor of traveling the country.

Clomid vs. Repronex

For over a year and a half, Chris and Christy have been praying for a child to be added to their family. They understand God's timing is always the best in the midst of medical treatments, but still remain hopeful for a little Tanner to join their party!

Dysfunctional Homes vs. Adoptive Homes

After working as a therapist providing in-home services to children and families, Christy was able to return to her passion of helping birth parents and adoptive families at Lutheran Family Services. She loves her job and strongly supports adoption!

Christmas gifts vs. Christ's gift

This Christmas provides us another opportunity to remember the amazing gifts of love and grace God has given the world by sending his son Jesus to forgive our sins and grant us eternal life in heaven. The Tanners pray that this is your vote in 2004. Christ's gift is always the winner!

A Year of Firsts

The Year of Firsts letters were written by my sons' families. It is an added twist to the monthly chronology idea. In comparing the two, one blocks in each month with graphics and the other presents a chronological list. This is a great choice for new babies or newlyweds. Family websites with pictures make a great alternative to sending pictures or printing them in the letter. Geocities.com can provide you with a free website.

STEP 1. GENERATE YOUR OWN LIST OF TOPICS TO BE INCLUDED IN YOUR LETTER.

FAMILY MEMBERS, FRIENDS OR PETS	EVENTS, TRAVELS, HUMOROUS SITUATIONS, CHANGES, ACCOMPLISHMENTS, ACTIVITIES

STEP 2. YOUR THEME IS "A YEAR OF FIRSTS."

STEP 3. WEAVE TOPICS INTO THE THEME.
Arrange topics by month.

2000: A Year of Firsts for Robb, Joni, and Boyd

JANUARY
Robb and Joni celebrated their 1st new year as parents (and Boyd stayed up to watch the ball drop)! After her maternity leave, Joni had her 1st (and last) day back to work as a software engineer at NASA. She enjoyed writing software for space experiments, but being a stay-at-home mom is even more fun!

FEBRUARY
Robb had his 1st day of work as a contractor for NASA. He was a mechanical engineer working on an experiment that will operate on the space station.

MARCH
Boyd got his 1st tooth.

APRIL
Robb and Joni bought their 1st house! It is located in Hinckley, OH, and they have been keeping busy with home improvement projects.

MAY
Boyd said his 1st word, "DaDa" (Mommy and Kitty followed soon after). Robb graduated from Case Western Reserve University with a master's degree in mechanical engineering. He built and controlled a one-legged walking robot for his thesis.

JUNE
Boyd crawled for the 1st time (and figured out how to get into everything).

JULY
Robb, for the 1st (and only) time, got to sit in the space shuttle that is used for astronaut training.

AUGUST
Robb and Joni experienced their 1st house disaster when the bathtub leaked through to the kitchen ceiling. They began fixing the tub, and 3 months later ended up with a completely renovated bathroom!

SEPTEMBER
Boyd took his 1st steps. Robb put the 1st wall up in his sound-proof recording studio, which he is building in the basement.

OCTOBER
Robb and Joni played drums and percussion in the praise band for the 1st time at their new church, Polaris Christian Church. They are now playing every other month.

NOVEMBER
Boyd celebrated his 1st birthday with lots of friends, family, and cake! After 25 years, Joni had her hair cut short for the 1st time. She had 17 inches cut off and donated it to Wigs for Kids, a non-profit organization that makes wigs for children who have lost their hair.

DECEMBER
After quitting his job at NASA, Robb had his 1st day of work at Codonics, a company that makes diagnostic quality printers for the medical industry.

More Firsts...

MERRY CHRISTMAS FROM THE COLBRUNNS!

As we come to the end of our first full year as a triplet family, we are amazed at how much things have changed. It truly was a "Year of Firsts." Here are some of the highlights...

January **First Smile.** Seeing your babies smile for the first time is worth waiting for!
First Time Noticing Themselves in the Mirror. Britany saw herself and said, "Oooh!"

February **First Laugh.** The antics of Mom, Dad, and the relatives are good material to make babies laugh!

March **First Big Night Out for Mom and Dad.** As a birthday surprise, Jonn took Jen out to dinner and a Steven Curtis Chapman concert in Ann Arbor.

April **First Time Rolling Over.** This quickly became their primary mode of transportation!
First Time in Church. The kids were baptized at Third Baptist Church in Muskegan, MI, where Jen's family has been attending for over 100 years.
First Stroller Ride. Our two strollers (one holds two kids) were used almost daily through October. A fun ride for the kids and a nice break for Jen.

May **First Tooth for Britany & Brent.** Ethan's first tooth came later — he was too busy growing out his thick red hair!
First Time Saying "Mama." They actually said "Momomom", but we knew what they meant!
First Boat Ride. Grandpa Anderson took us all for a boat ride on Lake Michigan.

June **First Time All Three Slept the Entire Night!** We had hoped that this would become the standard operating procedure, but no such luck. On rare occasions when this does happen, it is still cause for celebration!
First Trip to Ohio. We celebrated Grandpa Colbrunn's retirement and visited with family and friends on Jonn's side.
First Nanny. After having the Grandmas live with us since the kids were born (Jan & Barb switched every other week), we hired Alexandria to help Jen during the day. Margaret has been our nanny this fall.

July **First Time Crawling.** They started out with a scooting army crawl, but were soon moving everywhere. They especially liked to chase our cats!
First Time at the Beach. The kids enjoyed splashing in Lake Michigan during our week-long vacation with Grandma & Grandpa Anderson.
First Time Standing Up. Ethan surprised us all one day when he grabbed Great-Grandpa Anderson's pant legs and pulled himself up!
First Cold. When one gets it, they all get it. It makes for some tough nights for Mom & Dad. Thankfully, they have been very healthy overall.

August **First Picnic at Grandma & Grandpa Colbrunn's.** They had fun eating watermelon and playing with their cousins during the annual summer family gathering.
First Time Clapping. The kids enjoy clapping to congratulate each other and when they are listening to music.

September **First Shopping Trips.** We ventured out to the mall, Meijer, and Jen's favorite store (Gabriala's) with the kids, where they discovered it is a lot of fun to grab stuff off the racks!
First Trip to the Zoo. The kids enjoyed checking out all of the different types of "kitties" at the Detroit Zoo with our friends, Mark and Laura.
First Visit to the Apple Orchard. We went with Grandma & Grandpa Colbrunn to the Country Orchard for a wagon ride and pictures in the pumpkin patch.
First Time Out to Dinner. After the Baby Dedication at our church, we went to Red Lobster with the grandparents. Britany was the center of attention while Brent and Ethan slept through the whole meal.

October **First Birthday!** We celebrated their first birthday with the relatives at a Veggie Tales-themed party. The toys they received were almost as much fun as the paper and boxes they were wrapped in.
First Time Trick-or-Treating. A cow, a bunny, and a lion went to visit a few of the neighbors. Their mom & dad had to help eat the candy, of course!
First Kiss. All three kids gave their mommy a kiss.
First Big-People Food. The kids began eating graham crackers, and even got a taste of ice cream from Grandma Anderson!
First Words. Both Ethan and Brent like to pick up the ball and say "Ba!" and they hold the toy phone to their ear and say "Hi Da!" Britany likes to say "Baby."
First Time Up and Down Stairs. All three like to go up and down the stairs by themselves at the Anderson's. (They have plenty of them!) Each time Britany goes down a step, she claps for herself!

November **First Time Meeting Neighborhood Kids.** Every morning, the kids like to stand on the front window seat and wave at the school kids getting on the bus in front of our house. "Wheels on the bus go round and round..."
First Steps. All are getting steadier and are making progress each day. It won't be long before they outrun the cats!
First Cake. After de-thawing the cakes that they weren't interested in on their birthday, the kids thoroughly enjoyed it this time. It was followed up by baths for the kids and their high-chairs. Ethan may still have some frosting in his ears!

December **First Christmas Letter Written in a House with Three Active One-Year-Olds.** You're reading it! Thanks to Grandma & Grandpa Colbrunn for entertaining the kids so that we were able to write this!

You can see some pictures from throughout the year on our website: www.webaddress.com

May the birth of Christ fill your heart
with joy and peace this Christmas.
Happy Holidays!

Kid Quotes

Using the funny things that kids say not only makes a letter fun to read but can also give the reader a glimpse of the personality of the children. Explanations for what they say can include other family information which may not be caught directly in a quote. This is a good theme to use for a year when there is not a lot of family news to report.

STEP 1. GENERATE YOUR OWN LIST OF TOPICS TO BE INCLUDED IN YOUR LETTER.

FAMILY MEMBERS, FRIENDS OR PETS	EVENTS, TRAVELS, HUMOROUS SITUATIONS, CHANGES, ACCOMPLISHMENTS, ACTIVITIES

STEP 2. YOUR THEME IS "KID QUOTES."

STEP 3. WEAVE TOPICS INTO THE THEME.
List humorous things that were said.

Dear Family and Friends

We thought that we would share with you the things that we learned (or were reminded of) from our children in 2004:

So far we have been able to crack the code of their "triplet language":
- Bug cheerios, waterlemon, and wiggles actually taste pretty good. (Honey Nut Cheerios, watermelon, and finger jello.)
- Being called "Silly" is a term of endearment.

You never know what they are going to say:
- Britany exclaimed,"I'm busy!" when asked to wash her hands.
- Daddy said, "Mommy is powdering her nose." Ethan answered, "No, she is going pee pee."
- At dinnertime when Brent was not interested, he informed us, "OK, I'll come watch you eat."

Kids say the sweetest things too:
- Britany told Jana and Papa that her doll Elmo was going to sing a song to them on the phone. Britany then looked at her doll and said, "Go ahead Elmo..."
- Brent said, "Mommy sit on my lap for dinner."
  "I'm too big," I answered.
  "No, Mommy, you are just right," exclaimed Brent.
- On May 25, Gabe was born to Robb and Joni. Ethan said, "Happy birthday, new cousin." Brent urged, "Go see him!"
- On October 20, Kate and Brian's twins were born. Out of the blue, one day, Britany announced, "The pink one is Lindsey, and the blue one is Grant."

Kids are great imitators:
- All 3 have insisted, "Toy in time out for 2 minutes. Wait 'til it (timer) beeps."
- All 3 have pretended their toys were cameras. "Stand up, sit down, smile, back-up, cheese, smile, one more picture. See picture Daddy?" I wonder where they got that from?

Three year olds only have so much patience:
- On Thanksgiving, Britany informed us, "I can't sit here for like 2 OW ERRRSS!" (hours).

Don't forget the real reason for the season:
- When asked what kind of cake we should make for Jesus' birthday, the boys chorused, "Bob the Builder!" After all, Jesus was a carpenter.

We hope that their comments made you smile and laugh. You never know when you might teach a child something or learn something from him or her. We hope that you have a very Merry Christmas and enjoy spending time with your families. We look forward to hearing about your year and hope to see more of you in 2005. Our kids' website is: webaddress.com.

Love,
Our Family

Why Questions

Similar to the letter of quotations from the children, the "Why...?" letter offers insight into the family events and character of the children in a humorous and readable format.

STEP 1. GENERATE YOUR OWN LIST OF TOPICS TO BE INCLUDED IN YOUR LETTER.

FAMILY MEMBERS, FRIENDS OR PETS	EVENTS, TRAVELS, HUMOROUS SITUATIONS, CHANGES, ACCOMPLISHMENTS, ACTIVITIES

STEP 2. YOUR THEME IS "WHY QUESTIONS."

STEP 3. WEAVE TOPICS INTO THE THEME.
Recall any "why questions" that fit the category.

To Family and Friends,
The kids are learning their letters in preschool. The letter we hear
most is "Y", so we thought we'd tell you about our year
by sharing some examples of how they've used it.

BUT WHY?

Why is music class over?

Why are you building a bookshelf, Daddy?

Why does the sun go down when the moon comes out?

Why didn't God make me with 8 legs like an octopus?

Why is Papa standing on the roof? (He is helping us paint the trim.)

Why aren't cousin Molly's brothers the same age as her?

Why can't we go to swim class forever? (Finally warmed up to the idea on the last day!)

Why do they have a 3 person swing at gymnastics? (Perfect for a class full of multiples!)

What does Daddy do at work? I want to be just like Daddy. (I tried to explain it to him.) Quizzically, Brent looked at me and then said, "I'm just going to be a fireman!"

Why can't we play in the basement? (The basement flooded while we were on vacation which led to an impromptu remodeling project.)

Why doesn't our teacher live at preschool? (Well, at least not officially!)

Why did Great Grandpa have to die? (Jen's grandfather was very sick for 6 months.)

Why does my body stay here and my soul go to Heaven?

Why are you redecorating the office? (Making room to hopefully start baby books.)

Why can't we visit Strawberry Shortcake and Spiderman?

Why can't we see our new cousins now? (Christy, Jonn's sister, delivered twin boys on November 9. Their names are Brock and Garrett. Since they live in Nebraska, we haven't seen them yet.)

Why do we have Thanksgiving Day?

Why do we have heads? (They come with your body. It's a package deal.)

Why can't I get a real cell phone for Christmas?

Why does it take a long time before we grow up?

Why isn't my room painted yet? (We are attempting to paint and redecorate all three kids' rooms during this holiday season. Yes, we are a little crazy! Brent's room is Brent's Construction Company. Britany's room is Britany's Garden with ladybugs and Ethan's room is Ethan's Marina.

Why do we have Christmas?

Why did Jesus come to earth?

As you can see, some of these questions were much easier than others to answer.
We hope that you are all well and look forward to hearing from you.

Merry Christmas and Happy New Year!

Lessons Learned

The Important Lessons Learned listings entice the reader to read the explanation under each proverbial lesson just out of curiosity. A variation might include some lesson learned by each member of the family that year.

STEP 1.   GENERATE YOUR OWN LIST OF TOPICS TO BE INCLUDED IN YOUR LETTER.

FAMILY MEMBERS, FRIENDS OR PETS	EVENTS, TRAVELS, HUMOROUS SITUATIONS, CHANGES, ACCOMPLISHMENTS, ACTIVITIES

STEP 2.   YOUR THEME IS "LESSONS LEARNED."

STEP 3.   WEAVE TOPICS INTO THE THEME.
Develop "lesson statements" from topics listed above.

Important Lessons the Colbrunns Learned in 2003

- Joni can't be in a wedding without being pregnant:
  Since getting married, Joni has been in 3 weddings: her brother's when she was pregnant with Boyd, Robb's sister's when she was very pregnant with Lilia, and, in September, her college roommate's when it turned out she was pregnant with their baby who is due next summer on June 6th.

- Doorways in Japan aren't tall enough for Robb:
  This made for some funny pictures of Robb from his business trips to Japan. Fortunately, his other trips have been to Milwaukee and Chicago where he doesn't hit his head on doorways.

- No home improvement project is small:
  There's always a project going on in our house! The highlights from this year were having air conditioning installed (no easy task when your house has no duct work), designing and building a swingset/playscape, and waterproofing the basement (the rebuilding will continue well into the new year)!

- A pregnant woman needs more sleep than a 2-year old or 4-year old:
  Boyd and Lilia wear their Mom out racing, playing, and acting like siblings. Boyd enjoys drawing, singing, trains, action figures, gymnastics, Sunday School, and harassing his little sister. Lilia loves to talk, sing, dance, play with dolls, wrestle Boyd & Daddy, paint her nails with Mommy, and change her clothes often.

- Never ask a 4-year old to name a baby:
  After rejecting Mom's name choices for the baby, Boyd decided that since he already has a sister named Soggy O'Malley (his made-up nickname for Lilia), he would name the new baby Shoddy O'Roddy.

- You're never too big to enjoy riding Dumbo at Disney World:
  Everyone enjoyed our day at Disney while visiting Robb's college roommate and his family in Florida. The best part was leaving Ohio at 5 degrees Fahrenheit and landing in Florida at 90°F.

- Herbs really do work:
  After two pregnancies with hyperemesis (severe, all-day morning sickness resulting in dehydration and losing 20 pounds), Joni tried preventative herbs before this pregnancy. Robb and Joni have been pleasantly surprised by a healthier pregnancy with no hospital visits. However, Joni has been sick often enough that this will be their last baby (unless she's in another wedding).

- A sunset is beautiful, even from space:
  Joni viewed scenes from space and watched the astronauts aboard the Columbia through live video feed on the Internet. Part of their mission was running the experiment that Joni did programming for when she worked at NASA. In the end, though, we mourned the tragic loss of life from the shuttle's crash.

- God is always faithful, especially in times of sadness:
  Our family suffered a tragic loss when we lost a baby in June during a surprise pregnancy. Though our sadness is still there, we feel very blessed that the experience led us to the decision to have another baby. We were relieved during a recent ultrasound to see our active, healthy baby, and we were touched by God's mysterious ways when the doctor changed the due date to June 6, exactly one year after our loss.

Blessings

When we have had a wonderful year, a list of the blessings makes an easy format for sharing a family's gratitude to God.

STEP 1. GENERATE YOUR OWN LIST OF TOPICS TO BE INCLUDED IN YOUR LETTER.

FAMILY MEMBERS, FRIENDS OR PETS	EVENTS, TRAVELS, HUMOROUS SITUATIONS, CHANGES, ACCOMPLISHMENTS, ACTIVITIES

STEP 2. YOUR THEME IS "BLESSINGS."

STEP 3. WEAVE TOPICS INTO THE THEME.
Translate topics into "blessing statements."

Merry Christmas from all of us! We hope that you have had a year full of blessings! Our family has many things to be thankful for this year!

Robb received a promotion to Supervisor of Mechanical Engineering at Codonics, Inc. He even had to take a trip to Japan where he ate authentic sushi and was taller than everyone & everything (including the doors). Robb has also enjoyed spending his extra time (which there isn't much of) in our recording studio in the basement. We've recorded with friends, family, the church praise band, and even some up-and-coming rock stars.

Boyd turned 3 years old in November and his favorite question is 'Why?" His favorite things include drawing, making up songs with his daddy, his Thomas the Tank Engine trains, and playing with his little sister.

Lilia turned 1 year old in October. She started walking in August, and now she's trying to run after her big brother. One of her first words was "Bubba," her name for Boyd. Boyd wasn't too fond of his new name, so he decided to make up a name for her and announced, "If she calls me Bubba, then I'll call her Soggy O'Malley."

Joni spends her time chasing after Bubba and Soggy O'Malley, taking lots of pictures, and keeping busy with the Mommies & Me group at church. She's been using her college education answering all of Boyd's questions (including in-depth discussions on gravity and the vernal equinox). She has also enjoyed doing some recording in Colbrunn Studios under the label of Soggy O'Malley Records.

You're welcome to hear some samples from Colbrunn Studios and check out some pictures at our website: www.webaddress.com.

We wish you all a happy new year and a blessed holiday season!

Love,
Robb, Joni, Boyd, and Lilia

Family Statistics

A letter of statistics is fun to write for the mathematically inclined and fun to read for those who can't imagine what it is like to raise triplets. It is amazing how much information can be shared in this simple one-liner format.

STEP 1. GENERATE YOUR OWN LIST OF TOPICS TO BE INCLUDED IN YOUR LETTER.

FAMILY MEMBERS, FRIENDS OR PETS	EVENTS, TRAVELS, HUMOROUS SITUATIONS, CHANGES, ACCOMPLISHMENTS, ACTIVITIES

STEP 2. YOUR THEME IS "FAMILY STATISTICS."

STEP 3. WEAVE TOPICS INTO THE THEME.
Calculate statistics on topics from list.

Merry Christmas from the Colbrunns

We hope this letter finds you in good health and good spirits! As we think back over the year, we realize we can tell a pretty good story just by looking at some statistics. So here it is: "2003 by the Numbers."

260   gallons of milk consumed in our house this year.

572   loads of laundry done this year.

5475   sippy cups washed this year.

8740   diapers used this year.

45   hours per week that Jonn works as a Human Resources Project Manager for Visteon Corp.

98   hours per week that Jen works as a full-time triplet mom.

442   street address of our new house. We found a house in town with 4 bedrooms and more elbow room. We are definitely enjoying the extra space!

2   houses owned during the months of October and November. Special thanks to the buyer of our old house for not making this any longer!

72   hours for Jen and Mom and Dad Colbrunn to strip old wallpaper and repaint as we got our old house ready to sell.

0   rooms in our new house that we are planning to wallpaper!

7   two-year olds who celebrated their October birthdays together from the local Mothers of Multiples group. (Only 3 moms.)

2   great indoor playground locations in town that the kids enjoy. (Cookies & Milk, Jungle Java.)

3   times we visited the Toledo Zoo with friends and family. The kids liked the monkeys the best.

6   grandparents helped out all year long with projects around the house, moving logistics, and babysitting services. (We couldn't have done it without them!)

12   cousins and second-cousins that the kids had fun playing with on trips to Westland, Muskegon and Cleveland.

30   toddler teeth brushed every day at the beginning of the year.

60   toddler teeth brushed every day at the end of the year.

3   ducks in a wagon that went trick-or-treating in our neighborhood this Halloween.

9   other triplet and quadruplet families that will be riding with us on the Higher Order of Multiples float in the Christmas parade.

6   arms wrapped around us during a triple hug.

∞   priceless moments watching our kids grow up (too many to count).

1   reason for the Christmas season. We hope that the birth of Jesus has special meaning for you this Christmas season.

Best wishes for a Merry Christmas and a Happy New Year!

Sport Statistics

Sports enthusiasts will enjoy listing information about each family member in a manner that includes not only athletic accomplishments but also other events that can be tied in by using sports terminology. This same idea can be applied to any interest or hobby used as a Christmas letter theme. The terminology used in gardening, cooking, or computers can creatively be used to describe your family's year.

STEP 1. GENERATE YOUR OWN LIST OF TOPICS TO BE INCLUDED IN YOUR LETTER.

FAMILY MEMBERS, FRIENDS OR PETS	EVENTS, TRAVELS, HUMOROUS SITUATIONS, CHANGES, ACCOMPLISHMENTS, ACTIVITIES

STEP 2. YOUR THEME IS YOUR CHOICE OF HOBBY OR INTEREST.

STEP 3. WEAVE TOPICS INTO THE THEME.
List terminology that can be applied to topics.

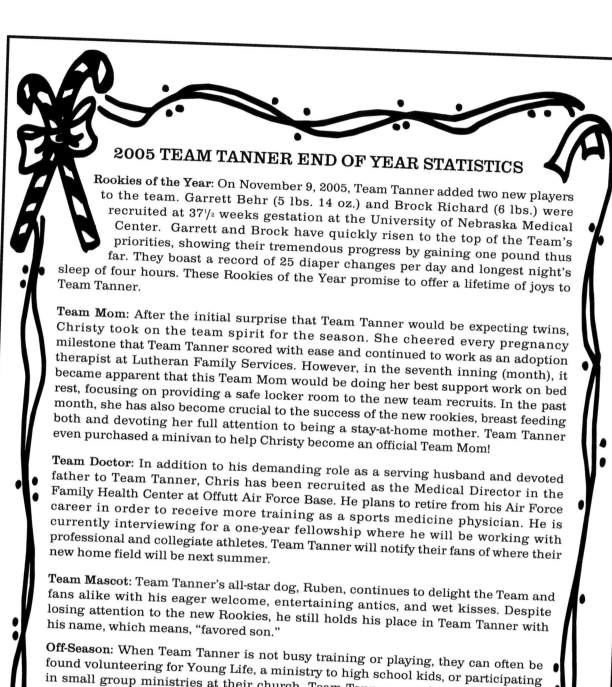

2005 TEAM TANNER END OF YEAR STATISTICS

Rookies of the Year: On November 9, 2005, Team Tanner added two new players to the team. Garrett Behr (5 lbs. 14 oz.) and Brock Richard (6 lbs.) were recruited at 37½ weeks gestation at the University of Nebraska Medical Center. Garrett and Brock have quickly risen to the top of the Team's priorities, showing their tremendous progress by gaining one pound thus far. They boast a record of 25 diaper changes per day and longest night's sleep of four hours. These Rookies of the Year promise to offer a lifetime of joys to Team Tanner.

Team Mom: After the initial surprise that Team Tanner would be expecting twins, Christy took on the team spirit for the season. She cheered every pregnancy milestone that Team Tanner scored with ease and continued to work as an adoption therapist at Lutheran Family Services. However, in the seventh inning (month), it became apparent that this Team Mom would be doing her best support work on bed rest, focusing on providing a safe locker room to the new team recruits. In the past month, she has also become crucial to the success of the new rookies, breast feeding both and devoting her full attention to being a stay-at-home mother. Team Tanner even purchased a minivan to help Christy become an official Team Mom!

Team Doctor: In addition to his demanding role as a serving husband and devoted father to Team Tanner, Chris has been recruited as the Medical Director in the Family Health Center at Offutt Air Force Base. He plans to retire from his Air Force career in order to receive more training as a sports medicine physician. He is currently interviewing for a one-year fellowship where he will be working with professional and collegiate athletes. Team Tanner will notify their fans of where their new home field will be next summer.

Team Mascot: Team Tanner's all-star dog, Ruben, continues to delight the Team and fans alike with his eager welcome, entertaining antics, and wet kisses. Despite losing attention to the new Rookies, he still holds his place in Team Tanner with his name, which means, "favored son."

Off-Season: When Team Tanner is not busy training or playing, they can often be found volunteering for Young Life, a ministry to high school kids, or participating in small group ministries at their church. Team Tanner especially loves their off-season where they travel to visit family and friends back East or explore new fields as far away as Banff National Park in Canada.

Most Valuable Player: When Team Tanner considers their victories in 2005, they must give credit to their Most Valuable Player, Jesus Christ. Team Tanner knows that His love, grace, and peace have supported them through the joys and sorrows of 2005 with eternal hope for the future. May you and your family also be blessed by this MVP!

Merry Christmas and Happy New Year from our Team to yours!

Best Sellers

The Best Sellers List was a really fun one to write. After selecting the topics, I wrote a short paragraph about that topic that resembled a book review. Next, I invented an interesting book title that reflected the main idea. The fun part was to create names for the authors that, when read aloud, sounded like a phrase that added humor to each book review. I remember lying awake at night trying to come up with a catchy phrase that sounded like a name. My daughter-in-law, Jen, came up with my favorite name: The author of the book about the never-ending Corvette restoration project was Carl B. Dunsoon. (Car'll be done soon.)

STEP 1.   GENERATE YOUR OWN LIST OF TOPICS TO BE INCLUDED IN YOUR LETTER.

FAMILY MEMBERS, FRIENDS OR PETS	EVENTS, TRAVELS, HUMOROUS SITUATIONS, CHANGES, ACCOMPLISHMENTS, ACTIVITIES

STEP 2.   YOUR THEME IS "BEST SELLERS."

STEP 3.   WEAVE TOPICS INTO THE THEME.
Brainstorm phrases that could be made into names for each topic.

Christmas 1996
Christmas Greetings from the Colbrunns!

We figured that by now you've grown tired of playing the Trivia Game that we sent you last Christmas and that you should be all ready to curl up with a nice book. We have some great recommendations from the 1996 Best Sellers List. So take your choice!

12. Housebreaking Your New Puppy by Willy Gough. A concise guide for teaching Daisy, a new Bichon Frise (little white curly dog), to mind her manners at home and away.

11. Restoring Old Corvettes by Carl B. Dunsoon. This unique guide describes how you can quit your job, hire lawn service, and work like a slave to complete what's suppose to be a fun, leisurely pastime. Maybe next year??

10. Long Distance Love by Minnie Myles Aweigh. This touching love story is about a guy named Robb who made up a song as a way of asking Joni to marry him. The heartbreak begins when he has to leave her in Grove City, Pennsylvania, after he graduates and goes to work as a mechanical engineer for Michigan Scientific in Milford, Michigan. Each week he longs to be with her, but there are drums to be played at the Sunday church service, CDs to record, a marching band to coach and tests for Joni to study for. We won't tell you the ending, but they're getting married next June.

9. Silly Sisters in Canada by Olive D. Gals. This thrilling adventure follows Janet, Arlene and Patty and their spiffy spouses on their first vacation together. They lived life on the edge of Niagara Falls and ventured into the depths of Toronto to take in a play, sightsee and shop. The real survivors were Donn, Jack and Phil who had to put up with the reminiscing and giggling. No violence in this one.

8. Dry Land Vacations Made Easy by Ida Rather, Bea Sayling. This vacation guide introduces the ultimate compromise for families which are too large to live on a sailboat. Renting a cottage on Traverse Bay and a Catalina 27 allows everyone including, Grandma, Tim, Jen's family, Joni and the Wagners to get in on the action on the water and off. The new girls in the family all passed the tests for sail-ability and late-night game-playing. Other very dry land vacations include seeing the Thompsons and Goodwins in Arizona, the Biggers in Tennessee and the Hawleys in Illinois.

7. Reach Out and Touch Someone by Colin Homalot and Hope E. Mayle. The heroine of this tale is named Christy. No matter where she is, some of her dear friends or family members are far away. The plot thickens as she tries to keep all informed about her life. Most of the time, she is studying psychology and business at Hope College but she ventures away for retreats with groups like Fellowship of Christian Students, Alcohol Issues Matter, Lighthouse Bible Study Leaders, and the college yearbook. Even when she worked at Boaters World this summer, she had to get away to visit her roommate in Wisconsin.

6. **The Phenomenon Of Reoccurring Appendicitis** by Dr. Belle E. Button. This is a scientific analysis of the underlying factors that cause three members of the same family to have their appendix removed in approximate five-year intervals. The case study includes Jonn, Jan and Robb (this year) and considers genetics, diet, environment and contagious factors. After a thorough investigation the scientists reached the same conclusion: coincidence. Regardless, Christy and Donn have committed to avoid long wilderness trips for at least five years.

5. **Looking Up** by Barry Short and Seymour Nosehair. This upbeat motivational guide follows the life of a guy named Tim. After working long hours as a store manager, Tim finds a new job as a marketing manager which uses his retail skills, has reasonable hours and great potential for advancement. He combined full time work with school for many years and is only a thesis paper away from his bachelor's degree. Things are definitely looking up!

4. **Recipes for Low Fat Computing** by Ima Ontheweb. This book tells you how to update your ware (hard, soft, flat or dinner) on a budget. First you shop around for a long time at computer shows for parts and pieces, because you don't want to make your mind up too soon or you might miss a bargain. Take one outdated computer, remove cards, motherboard and CPU in that order. Add a Pentium motherboard and 150MHz CPU, blend well. Stir in a new video card and 28.8 Modem. Bake well. Top with one of those free on-line discs. If you have any questions for chefs Robb and Donn, check with djcolbrunn@aol.com. Send us your address, too. Enjoy!

3. **Recognizing Your Friends at the 35th Class Reunion** by Hugh Gotta, Bea Kidding. The trick is to study the nametag while smiling about how they haven't changed a bit. The problem arises when only 75 show up out of a class of 600, most of whom you never knew anyway. Thank goodness for seeing Carol, Pat and Nancy who haven't changed a bit — really! The other recommendation is to take line dancing lessons so you can do the electric slide with the old people there.

2. **Going to the Chapel** by Mary and Will Bethere. This book will keep you in stitches as you follow Jonn and Jen around the country going to one wedding after another. They were the first among their friends to get engaged and married. Since that time, they have been to at least 8 weddings including those who vowed never to wed. It's a good thing for good steady jobs to maintain this addiction. Their other addictions include computers and playing fetch with Sneaker. Yes, Sneaker is a cat!

1. **The Bible inspired by God.** Still top on the Best Sellers List, this inspirational book explains the reason for the season: The birth of Jesus Christ, God's gift of love for the world! May you all enjoy a very Merry Christmas and a Happy New Year.

Notes

Use this space for your own List Letter theme ideas!

Consider developing a theme around…

    a shopping list

    places to visit

    who's who

    survival items

    things to do

PART III
Format Letters

Christmas letter readers don't expect to receive a crossword puzzle or a game in the mail from you that is filled with family news. Perhaps it is the element of surprise that gives the creative letter an air of anticipation. Some have noted that they enjoy sharing our letters with people who don't even know us just because they are so much fun to read. Perhaps, the next format theme lies on a shelf in your home where any printed matter may be found.

In This Section:

Crossword Puzzle

Yearbook

Diary

Game

Acrostic

Scripture

Santa Letters

Play-On-Words

Magazine

Newspaper

Dictionary

Crossword Puzzle

Developing a newsy crossword puzzle seemed impossible when I began. First, I had to develop a grid size and shape that would fit my letter format. I placed it at the bottom third on the back of the across and down clues. This allowed the reader to simply lift the bottom of the sheet and see the grid right side up for filling in the answers without seeing the key which was at the top. Second, I wanted to send a secret greeting within the puzzle itself. So I highlighted the spaces for MERRY CHRISTMAS and JOYFUL NEW MILLENNIUM. This became the core of the puzzle and I added words around them that somehow fit the information that I wanted to be included. You may notice that that Merry Christmas appeared in the shape of a cross; something that I hadn't even planned! Just to make it all work, I even spelled one word backward. I was surprised how many people reported that they actually worked the puzzle.

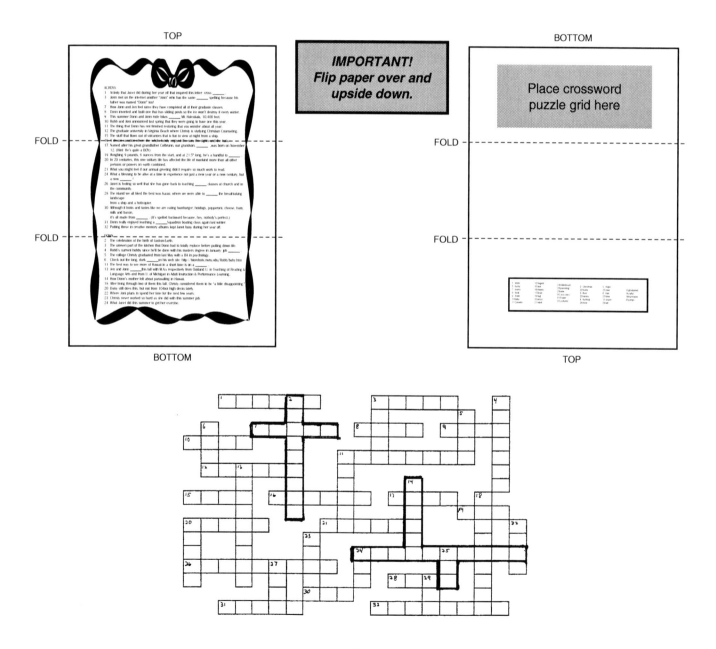

The 1999 Colbrunn Christmas Crossword

ACROSS

1   Activity that Janet did during her year off that inspired this letter: cross _____ .
3   Jonn met on the internet another "Jonn" who has the same _____ spelling because his father was named "Donn" too!
7   How Jonn and Jen feel since they have completed all of their graduate classes.
8   Donn invented and built one that has sliding posts so the ice won't destroy it every winter.
9   This summer Donn and Jonn rode bikes _____ Mt. Haleakala, 10,400 feet.
10. Robb and Joni announced last spring that they were going to have one this year.
11   The thing that Donn has not finished restoring that you wonder about all year.
12   The graduate university in Virginia Beach where Christy is studying Christian Counseling.
15   The stuff that flows out of volcanoes that is fun to view at night from a ship.
16   A dream vacation where the whole family enjoyed the sun, the sights and the hula.
17   Named after his great grandfather Colbrunn, our grandson, _____ ,was born on November 12. (Hint: He's quite a BOY.)
19   Weighing 9 pounds, 6 ounces from the start, and at 21.5 inches long, he's a handful to _____ .
20   In 20 centuries, this one solitary life has affected the life of mankind more than all other persons or powers on earth combined.
21   What you might feel if our annual greeting didn't require so much work to read.
24   What a blessing to be alive at a time to experience not just a new year or a new century, but a new _____!
26   Janet is feeling so well that she has gone back to teaching _____ classes at church and in the community.
28   The island we all liked the best was Kauai, where we were able to _____ the breathtaking landscape
     from a ship and a helicopter.
30   Although it looks and tastes like we are eating hamburger, hotdogs, pepperoni, cheese, ham, milk and bacon,
     it's all made from _____ . (It's spelled backward because, hey, nobody's perfect.)
31   Donn really enjoyed teaching a _____Squadron boating class again last winter.
32   Putting these in creative memory albums kept Janet busy during her year off.

DOWN

2   The celebration of the birth of God-on-Earth.
3   The uneven part of the kitchen that Donn had to totally replace before putting down tile.
4   Robb's current hobby since he'll be done with his masters degree in January: job _____ .
5   The college Christy graduated from last May with a BA in psychology.
6   Check out the long, dark _____on his web site: http://biorobots.cwru.edu/personnel/Robb/baby.htm.
11   The best way to see more of Hawaii in a short time is on a _____ .
13   Jen and Jonn _____this fall with M.A.s respectively from Oakland U. in Teaching of Reading & Language Arts
     and from U. of Michigan in Adult Instruction & Performance Learning.
14   How Donn's mother felt about parasailing in Hawaii.
18   After living through two of them this fall, Christy considered them to be "a little disappointing."
20   Daisy still does this, but not from 10-foot high decks lately.
22   Where Joni plans to spend her time for the next few years.
23   Christy never worked so hard as she did with this summer job.
24   What Janet did this summer to get her exercise.
25   Since Jonn's company lost their contract with Ford, he is looking for a _____ job too.
27   Janet loves being back to her counseling job this fall half- _____ .
29   What we did all the time on the cruise.

	Across			KEY		Down		
1	stitch	12	Regent	24	millennium	2	Christmas	13	graduated	24	mow
3	funny	15	lava	26	parenting	3	floor	14	joyful	25	new
7	merry	16	Hawaii	28	view	4	hunting	18	hurricane	27	time
8	dock	17	Boyd	30	yos (soy)	5	Hope	20	jumps	29	eat
9	down	19	hug	31	Power	6	hair	22	home		
10	baby	20	Jesus	32	pictures	11	cruise	23	nanny		
11	Corvette	21	relief								

Yearbook

Christy and I, both, had been yearbook editors in school. So, with her flair for layouts, we were able to include a lot of pictures and give our yearbook letter an authentic look. Printing on both sides of three half-sheets, we used a ribbon to hold the sheets together at the fold. A star sticker can be added to the top of the tree on the cover when the assembly is completed. The yearbook, as you see it on the following pages, is presented in reading order and not in the order that it must be placed for printing. The following instructions will help you place each page layout so it will read properly after it is assembled.

Instructions

1. A booklet format must have pages in multiples of 4 (i.e., 4, 8, 12, etc.).

2. Determine what will go on each page, keeping it the size of a quarter sheet.

3. Type the text and place pictures according to the diagram below for the 12 pages. If that is too complicated, you can literally cut and paste your text and graphics on the appropriate pages. In the latter case, you must then use a hard copy to reproduce your letter rather than a CD.

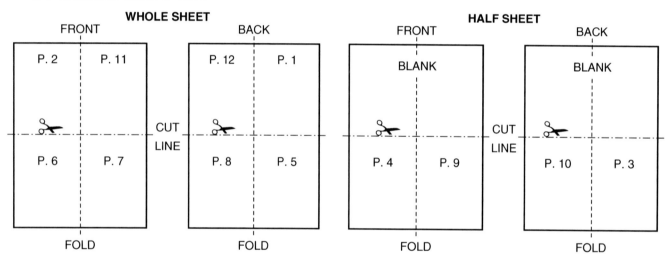

4. Copy both sides of each sheet.

5. Cut both sheets in half, saving three printed half sheets and discarding the blank half sheet.

6. Place pages 2 and 11 down first.
   On top of that place pages 4 and 9.
   Then place pages 6 and 7 on the top.

7. Fold all 3 pages together.
   Secure with a ribbon
   forming a book, or punch
   two holes on the edge
   and secure with a ribbon.

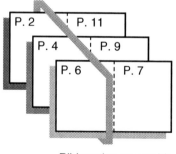

Ribbon ties on outside

Driving Miss Daisy – Crazy

Having four cats in the family has been quite an adjustment for Daisy, who, by the way, also enjoys walking on the back of the couch and sleeping on the window sill. They don't like her to chase them, but it's fair to play with her ears and tail when she is sleeping. It was bad enough to be the smallest dog in her obedience class, but to live in fear that these felines might eventually outgrow her is humiliating. There is no doubt that she is the baby of the family since she says, "Mama" when she wants to eat and is always looking for a warm lap to sit on.

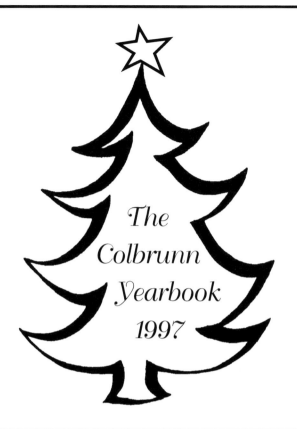

The Colbrunn Yearbook 1997

Dedication

This yearbook is dedicated to the friends and relatives who have supported us this year by sharing in our joyful times and praying in our stressful times. May you receive God's richest blessings as we celebrate the birth of our Lord in this Christmas season and throughout the new year to come.

A Retirement Preview

Getting a feel for what retired life might be like, Janet and Donn took an empty-nester vacation to Florida in the spring. They rented a house and sailboat on the intracoastal waterway for a week with the Geamans and the Haydens. They decided that it wouldn't be a bad way to spend retirement winters. Since Janet needed credits for recertification, she made the most of it by taking a 1-week course in June at a Rocky Mountain resort. Consenting to be a travel companion, Donn spent his days hiking, biking and white-water rafting. In July, they took Christy and Grandma to visit the Bollinger relatives on the Northwest coast, taking in Mt. St. Helens and the Redwood Forest. Even Donn's job has taken him on a new journey. He now has added responsibilities such as the Trip Captain. All this has only given him more homework and less time to work at home like on the 1961 Corvette. Carl B. Dunsoon was wrong!

Retirement Can Wait

The "aging" part of retirement began this fall for Janet when she experienced back pain during exercise. Ultimately, the cardiologist diagnosed some heart blockage and recommended the usual catherization and angioplasty routine. Thanks to the success of alternative medicine, she is taking chelation therapy instead and already notices improvement. This amino acid intravenous process is given once a week and opens up the arteries, rejuvenating the entire circulatory system. Chelation has been used for thirty years in thousands of clinics around the world and is considered safer than taking an aspirin. What an emotional trip that has been and thank God for the early warning. In four months the treatments will be complete except for periodic maintenance. She is grateful to be Bypassing Bypass and to be Forty Something Forever! (book titles on the topic.) She can send you more information if you know someone looking for a safer alternative for any kind of circulatory problem.

On the Move Again

Jonn and Jen had a big year of changes. Jonn is now working for MSX International, a supplier for Ford, designing training programs. Jen is teaching fourth grade in the Walled Lake Consolidated Schools. They bought a house in Warren, Michigan, about an hour south of the Clarkston Colbrunns. With all the extra room, they decided to get a second kitten, named Precious. She has been good company for Sneaker during those long days home alone. Jen continues to work on her masters degree in Reading and Language Arts at Oakland University and Jonn began a masters program in Performance Technology at the University of Michigan. In their "spare" time, they enjoy the many privileges that come with being new homeowners! Their biggest challenge will be to tame their backyard which is a perennial gardener's dream.

Hitting the Books – Extra Hard

Christy's fall semester as a junior at Hope College has been overwhelming with over 125 pages of reports and term papers written, heavy duty reading, science labs, projects, a practicum and numerous other extra-curricular activities. Last spring wasn't much better except for the two weeks off in March when she had her appendix removed. We're on a first name basis with the hospital surgery staff, especially with Dr. Belle E. Button who wanted her, after Robb's appendectomy, not to go off into the wilderness. She was less than a month away from a missions trip in the backcountry of Kentucky when the attack hit her. She even had homework last summer when she took an economics course at the community college while working full time doing data entry at Kmart International Headquarters. Christy does not expect the homework load to lessen anytime soon, as she was accepted to attend the Focus on the Family Institute in Colorado next semester.

Off to a Good Start

Robb and Joni courageously began married life together on June 7th with 16 children in their wedding party. After honeymooning in the mountains of West Virginia, they settled in a house that they are renting in Northville, Michigan, near the Warren Colbrunns. The former renter kept reptiles and Robb was fortunate to find the lost lizard in the basement, the day before the wedding. In similar manner, Robb's first brave deed as a husband was to lure a bat out of their bedroom one night. The kitten twins, Angel and Sunshine, arrived in September, to make sure that no more wild animals venture by. With a fresh degree in math and computer science from Grove City College, Joni found a job as a computer analyst with the Dow/Anderson Alliance. Robb continues to enjoy his work at Michigan Scientific. Sharing their musical talents, they are playing percussion in their church band.

Diary

The diary format was inspired by 11 year-old Christy who, indeed, wrote it in a dry bathtub while exercising her gerbil. We folded each sheet in quarters and used a folded sticker to give the locked book look. Computer graphics and small envelopes are much more readily available today. Kids may enjoy coloring the graphics after the copies are made. Some themes will carry over from year to year, like the Corvette restoration project.

This is how to layout a double fold (also called French fold) booklet:

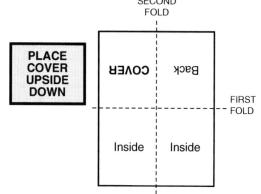

STEP 1. GENERATE YOUR OWN LIST OF TOPICS TO BE INCLUDED IN YOUR LETTER.

FAMILY MEMBERS, FRIENDS OR PETS	EVENTS, TRAVELS, HUMOROUS SITUATIONS, CHANGES, ACCOMPLISHMENTS, ACTIVITIES

STEP 2. YOUR THEME IS "DIARY."

STEP 3. WEAVE TOPICS INTO THE THEME.

Dear Diary,

This year has almost gone by and I haven't missed a day yet! I'm probably the only eleven year-old girl in the world who sits on the side of the bathtub each night with one leg in and one leg out to write in my diary while my gerbil, Chocolate Chip, gets his daily exercise running around in the tub and up and down my leg. I'm also probably the only one with my own secret code for things that happen every day, such as:

§ I still enjoy reading, dancing and piano lessons but synchronized swimming, watching little kids, and playing percussion in the school band are lots of fun too. Middle school is great with class changes and lockers, but sixth grade boys are disgusting.

★ Jonn has taken a new interest in girls and school activities since he got his drivers license. He reminded Dad again at supper how much we desperately need a third car.

◊ Robb never stops moving. He ran on the high school cross-country team this fall, and plays football with the neighborhood kids every night after school. Now he can't wait for enough snow to start skiing.

✳ Dad advised the boys to schedule some time to work on putting the old 1961 Corvette back together this weekend. They tore it apart this summer and I think he's afraid it will suffer the same fate as the Model A that has been half restored since B.C. (Before Children).

❖ Mom was either at a counseling class or meeting tonight but she got home in time to braid my hair in 14 braids to get that fluffy, frizzy look for school tomorrow.

✳ Grandma was at the senior center making plans for another dinner or trip, but she still had time to bake cookies today!

I guess we're having company tomorrow night. Mom and Dad found someone else willing to see our two-hour video of our sailboating trip in the Virgin Islands last June. Snorkeling in the clear water with all the colored fish was fun until Robb and Jonn saw a stingray climbing up our anchor line! We all had a good time even though we only got to have one shower all week. Actually, the only bad part was being trapped on a 31' boat for seven days with my brothers.

I hope that I get a doll again for Christmas. I wonder if Mom will use my gerbil to write the Christmas letter this year to wish all of our friends a blessed Christmas season. Just so she doesn't ask me to write it!

Good night,

Christy

Christy's 1988 Diary

Game

The game letter was a challenge to develop but quite satisfying to see come together. I was able to create a facsimile of a game board and find a way to convey the family news that tied into the game. It's good, once in a while, to make fun of yourself as in the directions on the game board. That gives people permission to skip over your trivia and know that you won't be too offended. The trivia cards (printed on green paper) were cut, stacked and tied with a ribbon before enclosing.

STEP 1. GENERATE YOUR OWN LIST OF TOPICS TO BE INCLUDED IN YOUR LETTER.

FAMILY MEMBERS, FRIENDS OR PETS	EVENTS, TRAVELS, HUMOROUS SITUATIONS, CHANGES, ACCOMPLISHMENTS, ACTIVITIES

STEP 2. YOUR THEME IS "BOARD GAME."

STEP 3. WEAVE TOPICS INTO THE THEME.
Select a game board location title for each topic.

3rd Rek Family Reunion	Panama City Beach, Florida	Mall Yep, She's Here	Fairview High School 1960	Hope College	Electronicsitis Recovery Room

Denver I.C.F.		Six In-Laws And A Truck
Real Job	GREEN TRIVIA CARDS	Memorial Rock Garden
Boaters World	**1995 Trivia Repute**	Beaver, Pennsylvania
Surprise Un-Birthday Party		Grandparent Prep School
Senior Survival Center	Parker Brothers presents this limited edition game of the year. Provide your own playing pieces, dice, play money and rules, and you're on your way to learning everything you ever cared (or couldn't care less) to know about the Colbrunns. Have fun!	Nashville, Tennessee
Promise Keepers		Stationary Race Track

Start Our House	Your House	Church	Empty Nest	Garage	Nykerk: Hope College Grove Aid: Grove City College

You're stuck between going to GROVE AID (benefit concert that Robb organizes and performs in) or to NYKERK (singing competition between freshmen and sophomore women) on the same weekend. Sometimes you just can't win! Do not pass GO. Do not collect $200.

Advance to BOATERS WORLD to congratulate our star-boarder (pun intended), Tim, who is recognized for being the youngest and most successful Boaters World manager in the region. Spend $200.

Stick around longer at cousin Corrie's and Christy's graduation party and it magically turns into Grandma Chamber's 75th SURPRISE BIRTHDAY PARTY with relatives from California, Penny and Candy.

Thrill to the challenge of going nowhere fast on Jan's treadmill and Donn's bike while watching Rush Limbaugh on TV. See who wins at the STATIONARY RACE TRACK. No $200 bets will be accepted.

Advance to PANAMA CITY BEACH for spring break where Christy and her friends, Christyn and Kristy, learn that they can even have fun with Mom and Dad as chauffeurs, chaperones and credit card holders. Pay $200 for each hotel.

From OUR HOME to YOUR HOME, we wish you the joy of winning God's gift of Christmas: eternal life through His son, Jesus Christ. Have a very merry Christmas!

Attend GRANDPARENT PREP SCHOOL with Jan and Donn to practice cuddling Jen and Jonn's new...kitty, Sneaker. Miss a turn to take pictures.

For an inspirational vacation, travel to DENVER with Donn and Jan for the International Congress on the Family where you'll meet James Dobson and other Christian leaders defining the role of the church to strengthen families and thus the nation. Collect 200 good ideas.

Visit Donn at the ELECTRONICSITIS (see '94 letter) RECOVERY ROOM where he finally made a decision on which CD player to purchase. Offer to sell him your Get out of Debt Free card

Advance to PROMISE KEEPERS with Donn and be amazed how 70,000 men at the Silverdome can get as excited about living out Christian principles as they do about seeing the Detroit Lions win.

Miss four turns in the GARAGE. The 1961 Corvette restoration project is STILL not done.

Stop at CHURCH where you'll find Jan and Donn in a two-for-one combination called Christian Education Co-directors. That's what you get when you cross a Sunday School teacher with a Promise Keeper. Feel free to leave $200 in the offering plate.

Go find SIX IN-LAWS AND A TRUCK to help Jonn and Jen move closer to work, Consumers Power in Jackson and Tuckett Christian Academy in Royal Oak. Collect $200 for the gas money you save.

Take an extra turn while you do family bonding at the 3RD ANNUAL REK FAMILY REUNION. You'll need extra time to talk to all 130 of them.

Advance to SENIOR SURVIVAL CENTER. You have just lived through yearbook deadlines, AP. tests, final exams, prom, graduation, and open houses. Miss a turn with Christy to recover.

Check out NASHVILLE, TENNESSEE to see if Robb has any job potential with Saturn next May. Pay each music studio $50 to let you try writing or arranging music for them in your spare time.

Robb is one step away from a REAL JOB with his summer engineering internship with G.M. He'll graduate in May unless he decides to drop engineering to be a carpenter and build houses for Habitat for Humanity in Virginia like he did during spring break. Rent is $200 per house if you land there.

Advance to THE MALL (any mall) to look for Christy doing her favorite thing: shopping! Borrow $200 from the bank.

Christy's idea of a real job is to be a cashier at BOATERS WORLD for the summer. It helps to have cousin Tim for a boss. Pay $200 for taxes.

Take a side trip to BEAVER, PA, to meet Joni, a really sweet Grove City College junior, otherwise known as Robb's girlfriend. Robb says she's good company so tell her you're "Just Visiting."

Muffy was put to rest at 15 years old in our MEMORIAL ROCK GARDEN. We'll skip a turn to remember her silly antics and cuddly personality. Yes, Virginia, dogs do go to Heaven.

Go back 35 years and reminisce with Donn at his FAIRVIEW HIGH SCHOOL class reunion. The Four Lads were there! (If you're thinking, "Who?" you're too young to be impressed, so you can miss a turn.)

Visit Christy at HOPE COLLEGE where she is majoring in psychology. She loves college life except for 20 page papers and early classes. Miss 2 turns to catch up on your sleep.

When your kids all leave home, move ahead to the EMPTY NEST. Do it fast! As soon as you start to enjoy it, they're home again.

Acrostic

The Merry Christmas acrostic could be done to any holiday word or phrase. It is quite easy to draw words from your lists as long as you are able to think outside of the box. Some of our most humorous entries were written out of desperation and revealed everyday items to which most people can relate — like 'RR' in the sample acrostic letter on the next page. It's fun to find "prophesy fulfilled" in reading old letters. Indeed, under the second 'M', the last year we paid college tuition was the year before I retired.

STEP 1. **GENERATE YOUR OWN LIST OF TOPICS TO BE INCLUDED IN YOUR LETTER.**

FAMILY MEMBERS, FRIENDS OR PETS	EVENTS, TRAVELS, HUMOROUS SITUATIONS, CHANGES, ACCOMPLISHMENTS, ACTIVITIES

STEP 2. **YOUR THEME IS "ACROSTIC."**

STEP 3. **WEAVE TOPICS INTO THE THEME.**
List topic words that begin with the letters in your acrostic word.

THE 1989 COLBRUNN CHRISTMAS CANTATA

(If you have trouble singing the words to the
traditional melody, just make up your own tune.)

M is for MARCHING BAND. This fall we were totally immersed in the Clarkston High School Marching Band. The boys practiced at least three times a week and we all attended the football games and band competitions every weekend. We were especially proud to see Clarkston place third in the state competition since Donn was the official equipment truck driver and pit crew member; Robb, who usually plays saxophone, was a bass drummer in the award-winning percussion section and vice-president of Band Council; and Jonn directed the 110-member band as the drum major.

E is for EXPERIMENTAL ENGINEERING Manufacturing Services, Donn's new group assignment at Truck and Bus. Donn's particular job is to supervise the wood model shop and the cad/cam interface department. This is where computerized designs become real three-dimensional prototypes. Donn says his job is Especially Exciting and Enjoyable.

R is for REPAIRS. This is the year that we repositioned the leaning posts on the dock, replaced the rotten wood floor and transom in the fiberglass power boat (that's a real trick), not to mention repairing the air conditioner, dishwasher, washing machine, jet ski, computer, and water softener.

R is for (you guessed it) more REPAIRS. Thanks to the wise guys with the baseball bats, even the mailbox that is mounted on a spring loaded post needed to be repaired three times.

Y is for YEARLY group picnics we host every summer. This year we crammed three into one weekend. That way we only had to clean the house once — or at least that was the way it was supposed to work.

C is for CHRISTY who gets less homework in the seventh grade and loves it. She's really into saving things. Her collections include: books, money, candy (a chocolate bunny ear in the freezer since 1986) gum, nails (the ones over 1/2 inch that her piano teacher makes her cut), teeth (two more to go), ticket stubs and dance costumes from the past five years.

H is for the great college HUNT. We have visited at least eight colleges this year. Jonn has narrowed his selection down to two liberal arts colleges in Michigan: Alma and Hope. He hasn't decided on a major yet, but seems to like history and archeology (a la Indiana Jones) best so far.

R is for ROBB whose Odyssey of the Mind team placed third in the state in the senior high division by using a cue ball to successfully perform 13 tasks in 35 seconds in a creative manner. After five years in OM, he has taken on a new venture — learning to play the five-piece drum set that he bought from his cousin, Matt. (Or did Tim and Corrie pay Robb to buy it?) He's really pretty good so that is no way related to the fact that six out of our nine closest neighbors have their houses up for sale.

I is for IRENE, better known as Grandma. When she gets tired of the noise (see R) around here, she flies off to another part of the country to share her cookies and hugs with her other grandchildren and 7 great grandchildren.

S is for STEVE who had fun this summer learning how to direct the marching band, life-guarding at the local racquet club and capturing third place sailing with his dad at the Cass Lake Regatta. He's really been busy this fall playing trombone in the jazz band one hour before school starts every morning (good thing he has his own wheels), taking advanced placement courses, keeping track of the money for National Honor Society, designing the senior sweat shirt, and giving presentations, along with Robb, to younger students for Just Say No Club.

T is for TRIPS south. In June, we helped some friends from church move down to Saturn country in Tennessee and then at Thanksgiving we visited Walt Disney World with the Weiss clan. Ten of us traveled non-stop for 20 hours to test drive GM's new 15 passenger extended G van. That, in itself, was a real TRIP!

M is for MOM who is still in school. She should be done with an internship in school counseling by June. Anybody need an elementary school counselor for next fall? Those college bills for the kids are probably going to continue rolling in until it's time for her to retire.

A is for the ANIMATED caricatures done by Jonn since we couldn't afford pictures this year. (See RR) If you wave the paper around, it almost looks like we're moving our lips, sort of.

S is for SENDING SINCERE SALUTATIONS for a SIMPLY SENSATIONAL SEASON of the celebration of the birth of Christ and His gift of love and SALVATION for us and for you.

MERRY CHRISTMAS (for horizontal readers)!!!

Scripture

The third chapter of Ecclesiastes gave us a "scriptural" format appropriate to share the passing of my mother who had been living with us for six years. Although the "time to mourn and time to rejoice" parts are the only phrases true to scripture, we chose other contrasting words for the rest to better describe our lives. Indeed, those two phrases gave the letter power and meaning. You may notice, when the letter is folded properly, that two more pieces of clip art will appear beneath the cutaway area. The font style of the scripture passage gives the front of the letter a sacred look.

1. The scripture is placed upside down on the top of the back page.

2. When the letter is folded accordion style, the scripture page lifts up to see the top of the first page. The bottom folds back.

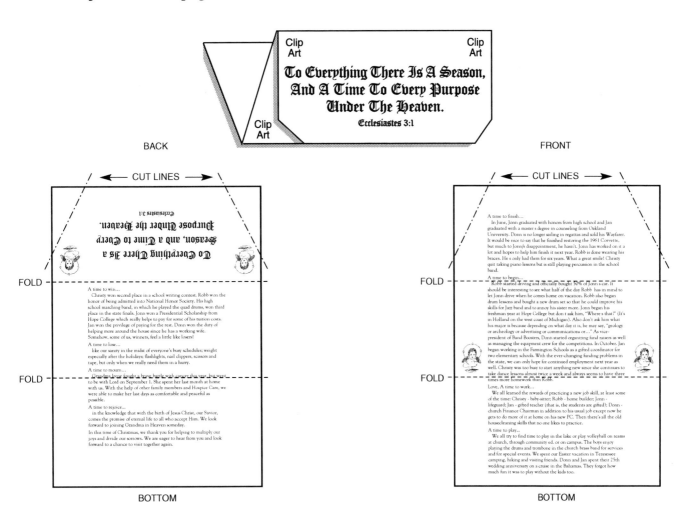

A time to finish…

In June, Jonn graduated with honors from high school and Jan graduated with a master's degree in counseling from Oakland University. Donn is no longer sailing in regattas and sold his Wayfarer. It would be nice to say that he finished restoring the 1961 Corvette, but much to Jonn's disappointment, he hasn't. Jonn has worked on it a lot and hopes to help him finish it next year. Robb is done wearing his braces. He's only had them for six years. What a great smile! Christy quit taking piano lessons but is still playing percussion in the school band.

A time to begin…

Robb started driving and officially bought 50% of Jonn's car. It should be interesting to see what half of the day Robb has in mind to let Jonn drive when he comes home on vacation. Robb also began drum lessons and bought a new drum set so that he could improve his skills for Jazz band and to annoy his sister more. Jonn began his freshman year at Hope College but don't ask him, "Where's that?" (It's in Holland on the west coast of Michigan.) Also don't ask him what his major is because depending on what day it is, he may say, "geology or archeology or advertising or communications or…" As vice-president of Band Boosters, Donn started organizing fund raisers as well as managing the equipment crew for the competitions. In October, Jan began working in the Farmington Schools as a gifted coordinator for two elementary schools. With the ever-changing funding problems in the state, we can only hope for continued employment next year as well. Christy was too busy to start anything new since she continues to take dance lessons almost twice a week and always seems to have three times more homework than Robb.

A time to work…

We all learned the rewards of practicing a new job skill, at least some of the time: Christy - baby-sitter; Robb - home builder; Jonn - lifeguard; Jan - gifted teacher (that is, the students are gifted); Donn - church Finance Chairman in addition to his usual job except now he gets to do more of it at home on his new PC. Then there's all the old housecleaning skills that no one likes to practice.

A time to play…

We all try to find time to play in the lake or play volleyball on teams at church, through community ed. or on campus. The boys enjoy playing the drums and trombone in the church brass band for services and for special events. We spent our Easter vacation in Tennessee camping, hiking and visiting friends. Donn and Jan spent their 25th wedding anniversary on a cruise in the Bahamas. They forgot how much fun it was to play without the kids too.

To Everything There Is a Season,
and a Time to Every Purpose
Under the Heaven.

Ecclesiastes 3:1

A time to win…

    Christy won second place in a school writing contest. Robb won the honor of being admitted into National Honor Society. His high school marching band, in which he played the quad drums, won third place in the state finals. Jonn won a Presidential Scholarship from Hope College which really helps to pay for some of his tuition costs. Jan won the privilege of paying for the rest. Donn won the duty of helping more around the house since he has a working wife. Somehow, some of us winners feel a little like losers!

A time to lose…

    like our sanity in the midst of everyone's busy schedules; weight especially after the holidays; flashlights, nail clippers, scissors and tape, but only when we really need them in a hurry.

A time to mourn…

    Grandma Irene fought a brave battle with cancer this year, but went to be with the Lord on September 1. She spent her last month at home with us. With the help of other family members and Hospice Care, we were able to make her last days as comfortable and peaceful as possible.

A time to rejoice…

    in the knowledge that with the birth of Jesus Christ, our Savior, comes the promise of eternal life to all who accept Him. We look forward to joining Grandma in Heaven someday.

    In this time of Christmas, we thank you for helping to multiply our joys and divide our sorrows. We are eager to hear from you and look forward to a chance to visit together again.

Santa Letters

Letters to Santa can fit any family but our teenagers had a ball writing their own. Jonn, our talented family artist, helped to pull the whole letter together with the cartoon that explains why none of us got what we requested from Santa that year. If composing on the computer, using a different font for each person adds to the impression that the letters were individually written. Each person could sign below his or her letter.

STEP 1.   GENERATE YOUR OWN LIST OF TOPICS TO BE INCLUDED IN YOUR LETTER.

FAMILY MEMBERS, FRIENDS OR PETS	EVENTS, TRAVELS, HUMOROUS SITUATIONS, CHANGES, ACCOMPLISHMENTS, ACTIVITIES

STEP 2.   YOUR THEME IS "LETTERS TO SANTA."

STEP 3.   WEAVE TOPICS INTO THE THEME.
Each person could select a "special gift request" that ties into their topics.

To the dear friends and relatives whom it may concern,

   Due to insufficient postage to reach the North Pole, these letters have been forwarded to you in hope of wishing you a blessed Christmas season and a prosperous New Year. Your letters to Santa may be sent to the Colbrunns who enjoy hearing from you.

Dear Santa,

Did you go to college? Let me guess. You majored in international aeronautics? Well, I'm really enjoying my second year at Hope College, but now I have to pick a major. I declared a major this fall in psychology, but I'm not quite sure. I would also like to major in everything else from geology to art history to German. But there's only time for one. So what I want for Christmas is enough money to become a professional student and major in everything. This would solve my problem! Now maybe I could help out a little financially since I've been working as a lifeguard all summer and as a Resident Assistant in the dorm this fall. If picking a career after college is just as hard as picking a major, I think I'd rather stay in college anyway!

Jonn

DEAR SANTA,

   I'VE BEEN BUILDING UP TO THIS ALL YEAR, SANTA – MY FRIEND AND BUDDY. YOU KNOW HOW MUCH I LOVE TO PLAY MUSIC ON WHATEVER – DRUMS, GUITAR, KEYBOARD. WELL, I HAD A LITTLE EXPERIENCE WITH HAVING SOMEONE DO A "PROFESSIONAL" RECORDING OF THIS BAND MY FRIENDS AND I HAVE. IT WAS GREAT! SO WHAT I'D REALLY LIKE FOR CHRISTMAS IS A RECORDING STUDIO. IT'S NOT LIKE I DON'T REALLY DESERVE IT. I WORKED HARD THIS FALL PLAYING THE QUAD–TOMS IN THE MARCHING BAND – OUR DRUM LINE DID TAKE FIRST PLACE IN THE STATE! AND WITH ALL MY HEAVY DUTY CLASSES THIS YEAR, I'VE ACTUALLY HAD TO STUDY A LOT. I DO REGULAR CHORES AROUND THE HOUSE AND I WAS ONLY A MONTH LATE IN GETTING MY APPLICATION OFF TO HOPE COLLEGE FOR NEXT YEAR. I EVEN SAVED SOME MONEY THIS SUMMER MAKING POPCORN AT THE LOCAL THEATER. THANKS FOR LISTENING, SANTA, DAD JUST LAUGHS WHEN I MENTION IT.

   ROBB

Dear Santa,

Just a little more time, Santa, that's all I need. Now we worked out the time issue concerning the housework since I started my elementary counseling job in Romeo Schools; everyone pitches in more. For one thing, since I'm in two schools, I just need more time to see the kids with problems individually and in groups. I like to lead preventative guidance sessions in all the classrooms too, with lessons on friendship, conflict resolution etc. But I'd really like to have more time for family activities. With the kids working in the summer and different times for vacations during the school year, we're lucky to get away to visit relatives. At least we all got to Warren in July for Tandy's (my niece) wedding. And we even made a short return trip to Lake Chautauqua in New York where we had vacationed every summer for twelve years. Instead of seeing the world, we brought the world home for three weeks this summer with a French exchange student, Raphael Lanoy. C'est bon n'est pas? The exchange part comes in February when Robb gets to go visit with him and his family for two weeks. If we could just make time to visit Hawaii. Let's see: round trip airfare times five, plus car rental, motels, and entry fees. Speaking of time, I'd better get busy on that Christmas letter. I'm all out of new ideas!

Jan

Dear Santa,

I have this wonderfully creative idea that you will just love. You know the little greenhouse that we have a bunch of junk stored in? Don't you think that would be a great place for a hot tub? Not one of those expensive ones, but just a glorified bathtub for two that circulates the water. Okay, even a 50 gallon barrel would do! Think of how relaxing that would be for you on Christmas Eve, Santa, to take a break in the warm water while watching the snow fall down at night. You can check my references. I've done well in school all year in spite of the frequent color guard practices in the Clarkston High School Marching Band which took second place in the state. Not to mention dance practices, being a counselor for sixth grade campers and a leader for preschool Safety Town this summer. Okay, Robb and I still fight, but if he didn't tease me... Now Mom thinks the idea is cool, but Dad is so practical!

Christy

Dear Santa,

I'll bet you're surprised to be getting a letter from me, Santa. But I just got wind of some pretty expensive requests, and decided since my name is on your credit card, maybe I deserve to have some input: Please ignore the above requests. Now I can identify with that lack of time issue, but I won't be Band Boosters president for much longer, and once the budget is done, the Church Finance Chairman job will ease up. But everyone forgot to mention the money issue. Let's see, 3 kids x 4-6 years of college x tuition + room & board, + or – scholarships, books, travel expenses, pizza, clothes... Well, Santa, you get the picture. But, if you really do have some connections, it sure would be fun to have a trailerable sailboat to tour the lakes up North.

Donn

Dear Santa,

My family has all gone crazy. Even I know that you don't exist. But as long as you make sure that there is a package of dog bones under the Christmas tree, I won't tell!

Love, Muffy

Play-On-Words Traditional Newsletter

Some letters that we have written have us rolling on the floor each time we proofread them. This was one of them. It appears to be a traditional Christmas letter, but subtly misuses sound-alike words in place of the appropriate words. We hope you can catch the thirteen proofreading errors. This is a difficult theme to follow, but a ton of fun to do.

STEP 1.   GENERATE YOUR OWN LIST OF TOPICS TO BE INCLUDED IN YOUR LETTER.

FAMILY MEMBERS, FRIENDS OR PETS	EVENTS, TRAVELS, HUMOROUS SITUATIONS, CHANGES, ACCOMPLISHMENTS, ACTIVITIES

STEP 2.   YOUR THEME IS "PLAY-ON-WORDS."

STEP 3.   WEAVE TOPICS INTO THE THEME.
After writing about your topics, select words that might have humorous sound-alike substitutes.

CHRISTMAS BLESSINGS

December, 1992

Greetings and Salivations from the Colbrunns!

The Christmas season has come around again and it is time to celebrate the birth of our Lord and to wish you God's blessings for a Merry Christmas and for a wonderful New Year.

Unfortunately, we got a late start so we gave up on coming up with a creative Colbrunn letter this year. So here I am, on the word processor, trying to complete a quick, ordinary run-down of our year's events before getting to bed tonight.

This year, I'll start with myself. I completed the school year in June with some concern for the security of my job since the school millage in Romeo failed. Nevertheless, my position as an elementary school counselor was spared and I was prepared to start school as usual in September… except the week before school started, I had to have my appendage removed. It's amazing how quickly an innocent tummy ache one day can become a serious condition the next. We thank God for a successful operation and a quick recovery with no concerns about workman's constipation.

Despite the condition of General Motors, Donn still feels relatively secure in his position with Truck and Bus (now called North American Trucks — no more buses) which continues to show a profit. Nevertheless, just to keep life interesting, in June he was transferred to the Milford Proving Grounds as Operations Support Manager. The people in the old department expressed their respect by giving him a plague when he left. He still has a passion for sailing and is planning a family vocation in the North Channel, the northern part of Lake Huron.

Robb was able to fulfill his wish in February to visit our foreign exchange guest, Raphael, in France for two weeks. He attended school there for a week, viewed the Winter Olympics, and toured Paris. He was quite compressed by the sights and crowds of Paris. He is now a freshman at Grove City College in Pennsylvania, majoring in mechanical engineering and unofficially majoring in music (marching band, stage band and Antithesis-his own college band). His music interest at home has still not ceased with a group called Onfreasonic. He and four other high school fiends released their second album in October. Robb will happily accept your orders at $4.99 (plus postage and handling)!

Jonn was also involved in international travel this year. He attended Vienna Summer School for three weeks in June and then spent ten days touring Germany with his friend, Jenny, and her family. He took pictures of the "Colbrunn Castle" and traced the Colbrunn roots, mating back to 1702. He is in his third year at Hope College with a psychology major and German minor. As a resident assistant and peer counselor, he has learned to helpfully listen to other's problems and has developed a keen sense of apathy. The guys worked on the interior of the 1961 Corvette this summer and predict completion in one to five years depending on whom you ask.

Christy is now finally in high school and loves being in the percussion section of the school band. She is involved in lots of clubs that meet before school in the morning. Not only does she enjoy the involvement, but Dad drives her to school on those mornings! She got her drivers permit this summer and is eager to jump into getting her divers license next summer so she won't have to ride the bus anymore. In junior high, last spring, she organized a new chapter of STAND (Students Taking A New Direction). She was also excited to be a representative to the State SADD (Students Against Drunk Driving) Conference this fall. She has given up dancing after twelve years but perspires to take figure skating lessons instead.

In case you think that our nest is getting empty, we have welcomed our nephew, Tim Swiss, to live with us so that he can attend Walsh College in Troy. He's great company and helps to reprieve Christy of some of the extra chores she inherited when her brothers left home.

Not all of us got to go to Europe but we did get to host two German students who were touring with a choir for a few days. Nevertheless, some of us (plus one friend) went to Perdido Beach, Alabama, last spring to boast in the sun. Others of us went white water rafting in July in Tennessee. We won't mention which one of us was too chicken to put her life in jeopardy but it wasn't Christy.

My goodness, it's 11:45! Spell check, print, and whoops... I guess I don't have time to proofread. Oh well, next year I'll be sure to plan ahead.

Magazine

Weather had been a big issue in 2004, so we decided to use a Farmer's Almanac magazine format. We made enough changes to the cover design to be recognized but not duplicated. To save on the price of color pictures of the grandchildren, we made a grid of pictures on our printer and cut and pasted them onto each card. We found that the internet was a great resource for tracing a vague recollection of the scientific authenticity of the Bethlehem Star. A magazine format was the perfect theme to include an advertisement for my not-so-soon-to-be-released Creative Christmas Letters book.

Instructions

1. Print the Back Cover and the Front Cover on the same side.
2. Print the two middle pages on the back of the Covers.

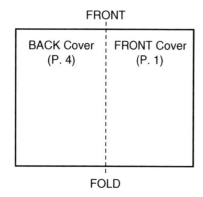
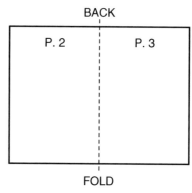

STEP 1. GENERATE YOUR OWN LIST OF TOPICS TO BE INCLUDED IN YOUR LETTER.

FAMILY MEMBERS, FRIENDS OR PETS	EVENTS, TRAVELS, HUMOROUS SITUATIONS, CHANGES, ACCOMPLISHMENTS, ACTIVITIES

STEP 2. YOUR THEME IS A "MAGAZINE" FORMAT.

STEP 3. WEAVE TOPICS INTO THE THEME.

Follow the format of the magazine selected.

ASTRONOMY

BETHLEHEM STAR — Researcher Frederick A. Larson has won acclaim from the world of science and theology concerning the astronomical legitimacy of the Biblical account of the Star of Bethlehem. Modern historical calculations determined the actual year of the birth of Jesus to be 2 B.C. Computerized programs that can project the sky, as it appeared over the Holy Land near that time, revealed that the planets, Jupiter and Venus, converged to create the brightest "star" that the magi had ever seen. Later, Jupiter appeared to stop over Bethlehem from the perspective of the Wise Men while in Jerusalem. Confirmed by astronomical history, this near-stationary position is called retrograde motion, similar to what we experience when we pass up a car on the highway. Larson also researched the Biblical reference to a blood-red moon-rise on the day that Jesus was crucified. Indeed, a lunar eclipse commenced before moon-rise on April 3, 33 AD, the crucifixion date based on historical evidence. See www.bethlehemstar.net for more details.

Indeed, the Star is not magic or a miracle, but more startling, it is the natural order that God put into place from the beginning. The life of Jesus is like a Christmas gift that if left unopened, has no personal value until we decide to accept and claim it as our own.

COMING SOON:
CREATIVE CHRISTMAS LETTERS
By Janet Colbrunn

A how-to guide to creating letters that will extend Christmas greetings while sharing the family news with a smile. This soon-to-be-released book is available to you for the asking, in appreciation for your accolades and encouragement during the past 20 years.

REGIONAL WEATHER

FLORIDA — THE SUN COAST
Winter: The weather was slightly cooler than normal, sunny and dry. It was a great winter for entertaining guests who were escaping the dreariness of Northern clouds and cold. Snowbirds found it a suitable environment for hunting for shark teeth fossils on the beach, playing tennis, biking, water aerobics and pinochle. It's a "together" lifestyle.
Summer: Very, very windy. Although four hurricanes ravaged Florida, the Venice area was spared from any major damage.
Fall: Sunny with ideal temperatures. A more leisurely time for the Colbrunns to complete the wall bed cabinet in the den, preparing for friends and family to visit.

MICHIGAN — GREAT LAKES COAST
Summer: The weather was cooler, wetter and cloudier than normal but it didn't get in the way of enjoying many family reunions. The Colbrunn clan got together in July to create a family video to send to Christy s husband in Iraq*. The family members starred as Olympic athletes and in some corny commercials. Chris loved it.
Fall: Consistent. Just like the other seasons, Jonn, Jen, Ethan, Brent and Britany enjoyed many activities with other multiples families. Jonn, since transferring to a job just 10 minutes from home, joins the family for lunch on Fridays. Newest challenge: potty-training triplets.

*IRAQ — ALL BEACH, NO COAST
Summer: Sandstorms, 120 degree heat, and no rain. Dr. Chris worked in a tent emergency room at a base in southern Iraq. In spite of the heat, he was a morale booster, organizing sporting events and leading Bible studies. He was able to visit Ur, Abraham s birthplace, which is located inside the boundaries of the base.

NEBRASKA — RIVER COAST
Winter: Cold, snowy. Great time for Christy and Chris to be busy in church and Young Life activities.
Spring: Cool, wet. Reason to escape to Italy for a 2 week vacation where it happened to be cool and wet.
Summer: No report. Chris was in Iraq from June to September and Christy was gone with Ruben visiting family and friends in Michigan, Ohio, Maryland, Virginia and Colorado
Fall: Sunny. Happily reunited, Christy took a job in adoption counseling with Lutheran Family Services.

OHIO — THE NORTH COAST
Winter: Cold and boring. Joni spent several months of bed-rest during her pregnancy. Best accomplishment: sorting Robb's screws, nuts and bolts into little tubs.
Spring and Summer: Wet and noisy. Gabe Joseph was born full term on May 25 but with immature lungs. After a week in the hospital, he came home to carry on the Colbrunn baby tradition of wakefulness.
Fall: Moderating. Getting back to normal life again, Boyd started preschool and Lilia enjoyed playing "mama" for her sweet baby brother.

WISHING OUR FAMILY AND FRIENDS A VERY MERRY CHRISTMAS AND A HAPPY NEW YEAR

Newspaper

The newspaper format is commonly used but was essential this time because my husband was determined to share some of his trip log from our North Channel adventures. We scaled down the font and squeezed in all the news plus some silliness just to keep people reading. Some computer programs help to format columns for you.

STEP 1.   GENERATE YOUR OWN LIST OF TOPICS TO BE INCLUDED IN YOUR LETTER.

FAMILY MEMBERS, FRIENDS OR PETS	EVENTS, TRAVELS, HUMOROUS SITUATIONS, CHANGES, ACCOMPLISHMENTS, ACTIVITIES

STEP 2.   YOUR THEME IS A "NEWSPAPER" FORMAT.

STEP 3.   WEAVE TOPICS INTO THE THEME.
Create article headlines for each topic to be covered.

COLBRUNN FAMILY TAKES ON NEW LOOK

Those who have not seen the Colbrunns lately have noticed that things are changing. Robb is now the tallest, Jonn is the heaviest, Christy is the blondest (but not the dizziest). Jan is wearing braces, and Donn is wearing glasses.

With a half century behind them, Jan said, "Old men are really nice!" Donn agreed recalling, "I don't remember my grandparents being so young when they were 50."

Another obvious change is an even number of males and females. Thanks to Jonn, next summer they will welcome Jenny Anderson into the family when his college sweetheart will become his wife.

Just two other changes: their new telephone area code is now 810 instead of 313 and their new zip code is extended to read 37400-5081.

Only Muffy has not changed a bit at age 13.

The Colbrunns (left to right) Jen, Jonn, Donn, Jan, Robb, Christy and Muffy

NOT ANOTHER FUND RAISER!

The Lord Mayor of Westminster has invited Christy Colbrunn and the 170 member Clarkston High School Band to march in the 1994 New Years Day Parade in London. Sixty-two bands from all over the world will participate in this week-long series of events. In addition, 80 parents will join their students on the trip which will begin on December 27.

For one year, the students and Band Booster parents have raised money for the trip through bottle drives, car washes, bake sales, candy and fruit sales, a dinner auction, gigantic garage sale, and a car raffle. Band parents, Donn and Jan Colbrunn, commented on looking forward to the trip if only to get some rest from fund raising!

COLBRUNN MISSES INDY QUALIFICATION

As a part of his new job responsibility supervising engineers in The Small Truck Test and Development Group at the GM Milford Proving Grounds, Donn Colbrunn was selected to attend the Bondurant Driving School in Phoenix. Although he was enrolled for the purpose of learning more about vehicle dynamics, he found himself wildly buzzing around the track in a formula race car along with other Indy 500 Wannabees. Other parts of the trip involved ABS brake testing in Death Valley. It's a tough job, but somebody's got to do it.

FRENCH TOURISTS ENTER SUMMER OLYMPICS IN CLARKSTON

The Daniel Lanoy family of Lyon, France, spent six days of their North American Tour last August participating in the Colbrunn Summer Olympics. This was the third exchange visit for Raphael who stayed with the Colbrunns during July of 1991 and for Robb who visited the Lanoys in February of 1992.

Raphael, his sister, Solanne, and friend, Pascal, won medals in backyard football, volleyball, water-skiing and marshmallow roasting. They also received world-wide acclaim for their cheering crowd role on Robb's latest band tape.

When asked about who had the most fun, the French or the Americans, the Colbrunns responded, "Oui," (we).

HOME ALONE CASE CAUSES PROTEST

Muffy Colbrunn has registered formal protests (mostly on Christy's carpet) to being left alone so much. "It's not bad enough that they're gone all day," Muffy comments, "but this marching band stuff has kept them busy all year with practices and fund-raisers and band booster meetings every week." Muffy has been assured that she will receive more attention following the band trip to London at the end of the year. Muffy's reaction was skeptical, "Right, they'll think of something else they can't say no to." Colbrunns were not available for comment. They were at a meeting.

SWEET SIXTEEN AT LAST

For many girls, 16 years old is the ultimate age. When asked what was so great about being 16, Christy Colbrunn says that it's as simple as A, B, C, D. "D is for DRIVING: driving myself to the mall, to school, to club meetings like SADD, National Honor Society, Interact, Blue & Gold, to baby sitting, to ice-skating lessons, and to volunteer at the Crisis Pregnancy Center. C is for CHOOSING COLLEGES. I'm starting to get literature from lots of them and making plans to visit. Finally, it's for me and not for my brothers. B is for BOYFRIEND. He's a Clarkston H.S. senior and we got acquainted last June when we both went to the 2-week Summer Institute at Michigan Technological University. A is for my GRADES. But don't tell anyone. It might sound like I'm bragging." Not to worry. Someday she'll wish she were 39 again.

WEDDING PLANS REVEALED

Jonn Colbrunn and Jenny Anderson announced their engagement on November 20 with 12:30 am calls to their parents. The young couple is planning a July 2 wedding in Muskegon, Michigan.

(Please see PLANS, 2A)

PLANS (from page 1A)

They will both graduate from Hope College in May of 1994. Jen will receive a BA in Elementary Education with a Language Arts Composite major and a Science/Math Composite minor. She hopes to teach third grade next year. Jonn will receive his BA with a major in psychology and minors in German and business. He will either be attending graduate school to study Organizational Behavior or will get a real job. This past summer, he completed an internship with Teledial in Grand Rapids. He'd like to finish the 1961 Corvette to take on their honeymoon, but it's not likely to go far without an engine. The interior was completed this past summer and the next mission is to tackle the brakes. Someday…

STUDENT ABDUCTED BY ALIENS

Grove City College mechanical engineering student, Robb Colbrunn, was abducted by aliens, forced to join a weight loss program and get a haircut. Actually, Christy did convince Robb that his hair was not cool that long, but the other bit of sensationalism was to make sure you continued to read the rest of this newsletter.

Robb spent his summer working for the township parks, baling hay and lining baseball fields. In his free time, he converted a damp and dark fruit cellar into a jazzy sound studio to record his band, Onfreasonic. They made a 60 minute tape of original songs and are selling them in a local music store along with a CD that they recorded at a professional studio. His other claim to fame is Whizbang and the Happy Jingoes, his college band that made a name for themselves playing for a benefit concert on campus this fall. Before you make fun of the name, consider that not many rock bands have a cello in them.

NORTH CHANNEL ADVENTURES

The following are excerpts from the recent best selling book by Donn Colbrunn. Colbrunn is presently considering offers for a movie contract based on this exciting true life adventure of a Michigan family's experience in a North Channel storm.

Donning foul weather gear, the crew of the sailboat, Figment, pushed away from the dock noting the dark skies in the west and headed for the open sea. Their destination was the Benjamin Islands, the jewels of the North Channel. The other sailors, looking at the rain clouds, said, "No way!" as they checked to see that their hatches were sealed tightly.

The expedition began on July 25th when the Colbrunn family and nephew, Tim Swiss, chartered a 35' O'Day sailboat out of Gore Bay in the North Channel. The channel is located at the top of Lake Huron and was formed by a large island, Manitoulin, and the Ontario mainland. Toward the eastern end there are many islands that make this area ideal for cruising. The Colbrunns had plotted a course that took them across the channel to the north side then eastward to the town of Little Current and then westward back to Gore Bay.

Navigation was the main focus when sailing since the glaciers had left many large boulders just a few feet under the surface of the water. Thanks to Tim's GPS (Global Positioning System) device, the Colbrunns never got lost or hit a rock. Every day they would sail to a new location, anchor in a bay for the night, and then explore the area. The scenery and views were spectacular and the hiking trails were plentiful. As time went on, the women folk began savoring the thought of warm showers in the town of Little Current instead of bathing in the cold lake water. The evening time brought out the card games and a lot of laughs, which is what Jan enjoyed the most. More interested in shopping, Christy was quoted saying, "You see one rocky island and you have seen them all." The "old salts" (men folk) enjoyed the sailing in stiff breezes and the rolling waves. Robb was very adept at finding all the blueberries on the trails.

Motoring westward with the wind on their nose, the sailors noticed the town of Little Current beginning to fade into the horizon. The sky was getting darker, the breeze stiffened and the rain began to fall. Donn began to wonder, "Did anyone ever think of putting windshield wipers on bifocal glasses?" Soon it was time to change to a northerly course. "Raise the sails," shouted Jonn. With Robb on the wheel, the crew scampered up on the deck to untie the sail from the boom and heaved on the halyard to raise it into place. The ship heeled to leeward as the sail filled. As the boat surged ahead, the crew's adrenaline continued to flow when they felt the full sensation of sailing. "Seven knots! We just hit seven knots." yelled Tim as the boat raced through the surf.

Tacking back and forth for over an hour, the crew worked the boat past Claperton Island and toward the Benjamins. Soon the navigator yelled, "That's Secretary Island straight ahead. Pass it to the left and stay 600 feet from its shore to miss the rocks to the west." With the sails down, the crew motored the final distance to the protected bay between the North and South Benjamin Islands. After throwing out the hook, the crew finally could relax. Everyone felt a sense of accomplishment and were rewarded with clearing skies. "I wonder if all those sailors tied up at the dock in Little Current were bored today," pondered Jonn.

EDITORIAL: WHY A CHRISTMAS?

As Christians throughout the world celebrate the birth of Jesus, we struggle to bring life and new meaning to the significance of Christmas. It seems that the more we learn about the intricacies of human life, the more we realize that it would take much more faith to believe in evolution than in creationism. To believe that life evolved from chaos would compare to a tornado whizzing through a junk yard of airplane parts to form a fully operable 747 airplane. And if God cared enough to form this Earth, why wouldn't He care enough to send His son to save us! It would be like trying to tell a bird where to find shelter from a storm. Only by becoming a bird, ourselves, could we adequately communicate our message and our concern.

We pray that this Christmas, you and your loved ones find new meaning and life in the birth of Jesus Christ, as a source of guidance and strength today and as a hope for eternal life.

…and Happy New Year!
From Our Editorial Staff

Dictionary

The dictionary idea is a good one to use when you have a wide variety of activities and situations to share. We had a lot to be proud of that year which might have come across like bragging in a conventional letter. Having more than one definition for each term gave us increased opportunity to be humorous, thus softening that boastful impression. This letter folds in thirds with the picture appearing when you open the title page.

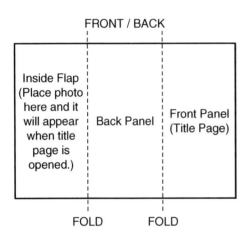

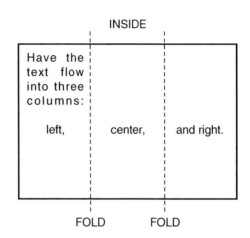

STEP 1.   GENERATE YOUR OWN LIST OF TOPICS TO BE INCLUDED IN YOUR LETTER.

FAMILY MEMBERS, FRIENDS OR PETS	EVENTS, TRAVELS, HUMOROUS SITUATIONS, CHANGES, ACCOMPLISHMENTS, ACTIVITIES

STEP 2.   YOUR THEME IS A "DICTIONARY" FORMAT.

STEP 3.   WEAVE TOPICS INTO THE THEME.

Select words or phrases from topics and develop real as well as humorous definitions.

Colbrunn Dictionary of Terms

1994
Christmas Edition

- 21 Entries
- Most up-to-date
- Easy to read type
- Over 5 million copies sold
- Low price of $5.95

Dedication

To the many friends and relatives of the Colbrunns
who every year sit on
pins and needles wondering what kind of
strange Christmas letter they
will receive as a way of wishing them a
Merry Christmas and a Happy New Year
without boring them to death.

See Wedding Festivities

ABS BRAKE HOT WEATHER TEST 1) When a GM engineer tests trucks in Death Valley in the midst of summer, with the option of staying in Las Vegas and visiting the Grand Canyon and Phoenix with his wife. 2) Another tough job that someone has to do.

ANDERSEN CONSULTANT 1) A person like Jonn, who has a degree in psychology, was hired for computer programming, is being groomed for Change Management, but is still waiting for a real assignment in the Detroit area. 2) One lucky college graduate who actually found a job.

BAND BOOSTER WITHDRAWAL 1) After spending eight years attending band booster meetings on Monday nights, and devoting untold hours, days, and weeks in fundraising and equipment moving, Donn and Jan wonder what else they will possibly do next year in their empty nest. 2) A not too painful process.

BENIGN SENIORITIS 1) When Christy cares more about being with her friends, having parties, and going shopping than studying, but is able to maintain a 4.0.

BONUS MONEY 1) The regular salary received by Jan, an elementary counselor, who loves the variety of working with kids, teachers and parents and would do it for free. 2) A bit of confidential information not to be divulged to her employer.

COLBRUNN INN 1) Where the driveway is always full and people come and go so much that some have stopped to check what we are dealing in. 2) An inexpensive place for Jen and Jonn to stay between the honeymoon and the new apartment in Utica, just 30 minutes away. 3) Where Robb spends his time in the summer when he is not working at Michigan Scientific or playing his guitar at the L.A. Cafe. 4) The last year for Christy where Mom, the maid, does her laundry. 5) Tim's home away from home while he is completing college and managing a Boater's World store. 6) Available for friends and relatives who can make reservations by calling 810-373-7400.

COLLEGE SEARCH 1) A quick stop at Wheaton College in April. 2) Visitation Day at Grove City College in September. 3) Scholars Day at Hope College in December. 4) A mad rush to get the application essays done before the end of the year between homework and extra-curricular activities.

DOUBLE TROUBLE 1) When Christy and her look-alike friend, Kristy, are dating the Sanford twins who are able to fool people by trading places.

EARLY 1994 NEW YEAR 1) That which occurred in London, England, while Donn and Jan were chaperoning 170 band members who got lost on the underground tube while shopping in the rain, marching in the cold and having a jolly good time.

ELECTRONICSITIS 1) A disease suffered by middle-aged men who are interested in shopping for the latest technology in computers, sound systems and cars but never quite ready to fork over the cash to buy them for fear that something better is about to be marketed.

ESCAPE FROM REAL SUMMER JOB 1) Occasional baby sitting. 2) Yearbook camp where editor, Christy, was sent and earned first place awards for layout design and theme. 3) A week at Girls State. 4) A week at Band Camp. 5) A busy volunteer counselor for 3 weeks with Campfire Boys and Girls.

ETERNITY LIFE INSURANCE 1) The belief that Jesus Christ really is the Son of God, born on Christmas, died and rose again on Easter. 2) Dividends of joy and peace receivable now. 3) The only life insurance that is redeemed by the deceased.

FINANCIAL REPRIEVE 1) The graduation of # 1 son from Hope College leaving only one Grove City tuition to pay until fall rolls around next year.

GROVE AID 1) Concert at Grove City College to raise funds for local food banks. 2) Reason that Robb had no time to do his homework for a week because he was busy conducting auditions and setting up the sound system as an officer in the Student Musicians Association.

HANGING IN THERE WITH SPUNK 1) What a dog named Muffy does, who is 98 years old in dog years, toothless, hard of hearing, and has cataracts, but still runs around acting silly. 2) What we have to look forward to in our old age.

INTERNATIONAL KIDNAPPING 1) Abduction of Donn Colbrunn and Jim Geaman to Toronto where they were released by their wives without ransom to attend Phantom of the Opera. 2) Adventuresome way to celebrate a 29th anniversary.

ONE ROOM SCHOOLHOUSE 1) A private school in Romeo where Jen teaches 21 students in grades kindergarten through fifth grade who are mostly boys. 2) A place where one very busy teacher works.

POLITICALLY INCORRECT 1) Traditional family values. 2) The dangers of pornography. 3) Corruptive effect of the media on children. 4) Value in the life of pre-borns, diseased, and handicapped. 5) Chastity and monogamy. 6) Treating evangelical Christians with the same tolerance and respect that other minorities receive. 7) Issues dealt with by Jan as the church Social Action ~~Chairman Chairwoman~~ Chairperson.

PRINCE ROBB 1) The honor of being invited to escort a Grove City College senior who was elected to be on the Homecoming Queen's Court. 2) An honor he almost forgot to tell his parents about.

WEDDING FESTIVITIES 1) Weeks and months of planning and shopping and reserving and preparing by Jonn and Jen, resulting in showers and gifts and a ceremony and reception on July 2. 2) An excuse to take a honeymoon on Mackinac Island. 3) A reason for Christy to be a bridesmaid. 4) A chance for Robb to give an original musical toast as best man. 5) A great way to get to see relatives and old-time friends in one place at one time.

WISHING YOU ALL THE MERRIEST OF CHRISTMASES AND THE HAPPIEST OF NEW YEARS 1) A Christmas greeting from Donn, Jan, Christy, Robb, Jonn and Jen. 2) Muffy too.

Notes

Use this space for your own Format Letter theme ideas!

To prime your imagination, consider…

   an event program

   compaign ads

   commercials

   a fairy tale

   a song

   a poem

PART IV
Perspective Letters

Writing a letter from a different perspective challenges the writer to not only report the family happenings, but to do so in a manner that captures the reader's imagination. In the world of Creative Christmas Letter-writing, any unlikely creature or thing could provide you with a pen name. Fortunately, you are not even limited by time and space. Letters from the future to the past, or from the heavens to the middle earth, can delight your imaginative friends.

In This Section:

Guardian Angel Perspective

Perspective of 100 Years Ago

House Perspective

Family Pet Perspective

Child's Perspective

Guardian Angel Annual Report to God

This letter is the only one that actually qualifies to be in all three categories of Christmas letters. It is written from the perspective of the Colbrunn guardian angel using an e-mail format, and listing the easy and hard jobs contained in the annual report. Since it was written on plain computer paper, I took the opportunity to enclose it in leftover Christmas cards I wanted to utilize. The angel communication to God was a perfect way to include particular prayer requests for the coming year.

STEP 1. GENERATE YOUR OWN LIST OF TOPICS TO BE INCLUDED IN YOUR LETTER.

FAMILY MEMBERS, FRIENDS OR PETS	EVENTS, TRAVELS, HUMOROUS SITUATIONS, CHANGES, ACCOMPLISHMENTS, ACTIVITIES

STEP 2. THIS THEME IS FROM THE PERSPECTIVE OF A GUARDIAN ANGEL.

STEP 3. WEAVE TOPICS INTO THE THEME.
List how answered prayers and praises tie into your topics.

Earthlink E-Mail/wishingyouamerrychristmasandahappynewyear.com

To: GOD@HEAVENLINK.COM
          cc: family and friends
From: colbrunnguardianangel@earthlink.com
Subject: Annual Report
Date: December 2005

Well, Lord, this has been an interesting year with many unique events that most normal families never encounter. Now I know why you gave me this assignment. Although some jobs were pretty (angel hair) hairy, other jobs were a piece of (angel food) cake. Pardon the puns, Lord, but I've been hovering around Donn too long.

Easy Jobs:

- Helping to provide sunny days to entertain family and friends in Florida.
- Providing safe travel on their 40th anniversary repeat honeymoon trip despite Donn's tendency to take the mountain curves fast in the Corvette. They didn't remember much from the first time, even though they stayed at three of the same motels. One of the other motels was in a sad state of disrepair and another was in a state of demolition. Indeed, some things had changed, but mostly they just can't remember much anymore. I'm not sure if even I can help with that one!
- Helping the kids to come up with clever excuses in order to get Donn and Jan to come to a surprise 40th anniversary party in July. Please forgive them, Lord, for all those lies. They also celebrated their anniversary with 10,000 Clarkston residents as they drove their original honeymoon car, the 1961 Corvette, in the 4th of July parade.
- Assuring the grandchildren that leaving Mommy is fun. Boyd loves kindergarten and can be found on the carpet reading books to his friends during free time. Brent, Ethan and Britany are real sweethearts and are enjoying their two mornings at preschool almost as much as Jen. Lilia is a natural dancer and never stops smiling in her ballet class.

Hard Jobs:

- Protecting Jonn and Donn as they climbed the 30-foot ladder to paint the trim on Jonn's house. Since fools rush in where angels fear to "climb," I convinced them to hire it done next time. Donn's going to stick to bathroom remodeling instead.
- Enabling Chris and Christy to conceive twin boys who were born on November 9 at 37.5 weeks. Garrett and Brock, at 6 pounds each, were named after me, Angel Babies, because they carried, delivered, and now eat and sleep in textbook fashion. Thank you, Lord, for answering their fervent prayers for babies with good dispositions.
- Holding Donn back from migrating to Florida in October would have normally been an insurmountable challenge, Lord, but going to Twinsville for an extensive heaven-sent mission with the babies was a beneficial alternative. Just ask Christy. Jonn and Jen insisted that Donn and Jan are overqualified after their triplet experiences.
- Diagnosing and sustaining 18-month old Gabe, who has allergies severe enough to cause asthmatic symptoms at times. Please keep him healthy this winter, Lord. He's one of your sweet angels.
- Arranging for Robb to find fulfillment in his new job at the Cleveland Clinic Research Laboratory. He is now a biomedical engineer currently working on knee issues.
- Accompanying Robb and Joni's 10-week old pre-born baby into the arms of Jesus. What an assurance that Christians enjoy, to see each other again in Heaven! Thanks for sending Christ to Earth on Christmas to offer that promise to all who seek Him.

Respectfully submitted,
Colbrunn Guardian Angel

http://www.3in1/godis2good2b4got10/jesusisthereason4theseason/rufeelingmt?theholyspiritcanfillthatgodshapedvacuuminsideofu.

Perspective of 100 Years Ago

It's amazing what inspires a theme for a Christmas letter. With all these new little Colbrunns to show off, I really wanted to put in a picture. Printing a color picture with the 120 letters that we usually send would have been quite expensive. An alternative, that would not be as costly, would be to print them one-by-one on our home computer printer. So, not wanting to appear cheap, I decided to do a black and white photo from an era when black and white was all there was. Not only that, but if the kids didn't smile, they would fit right in with the 1902 stoic-looking adults in the picture. Later, we did have a studio picture taken in color and put it on our website. The challenge then was to compare the twentieth century Colbrunns with the the twenty-first century Colbrunns. The only way to make it newsworthy was to say what would NOT be going on in our lives from the perspective of a hundred years ago.

STEP 1. GENERATE YOUR OWN LIST OF TOPICS TO BE INCLUDED IN YOUR LETTER.

FAMILY MEMBERS, FRIENDS OR PETS	EVENTS, TRAVELS, HUMOROUS SITUATIONS, CHANGES, ACCOMPLISHMENTS, ACTIVITIES

STEP 2. THIS THEME IS FROM THE PERSPECTIVE OF 100 YEARS AGO.

STEP 3. WEAVE TOPICS INTO THE THEME.

Start by listing what one topic could not be true 100 years ago for each person. The rest of the topics could fit under the current year.

IF WE WERE LIVING 100 YEARS AGO, ONLY ONE THING WOULD STILL BE THE SAME:

THE COLBRUNN CLAN WOULD STILL BE JOYOUSLY CELEBRATING THE BIRTH OF JESUS AND WISHING YOU A MERRY CHRISTMAS SEASON.

Christy, Chris, Noreen, Donn, Janet, Joni, Robb, Jonn, Jen, Lilia, Boyd, Ethan, Brent, Britany

IN 1902

- Donn would not have accepted an early retirement from GM. (Gus's Mercantile?)
- Janet would not be retired from a career as a school counselor.
- Jonn and Jen would not have been able to eat a peaceful dinner all year without their Baby Einstein DVDs to entertain the triplets.
- Robb and Joni would not have been able to record a CD in their studio featuring original music by family and friends.
- Christy would not be working at Bethany Christian Services helping with adoptions.
- Chris would not have been able to join the other 20,000 runners in the Marine Corps Marathon.
- Gramma Noreen would not have been able to take the inside passage cruise to Alaska with Janet and Donn without having been labeled a gold rush stampeder.
- The 1930 Model A, waiting for the past 30 years for Donn to continue the restoration project, would have been a future concept car.

IN 2002

Donn is busier than ever, working on home projects not only at our home but at Jonn's and Robb's as well. He also spent two months this summer coordinating a church remodeling project. One day a week, we still help Jen with the triplets, while she has the help of a nanny on the other four. We are still wondering if the job will get easier or harder as Britany, Brent, and Ethan become more skillful at walking and exploring. We make frequent trips to Ohio where Lilia is learning to talk and Boyd is learning to tease. Since he doesn't like her calling him 'Bubba', he calls her 'Soggy O Malley'. We're proud that Robb was promoted to Supervisor of Mechanical Engineering at Codonics. We look forward to learning where the Air Force will be sending Chris and Christy for the next 3 years, knowing it would be our next travel destination. Somewhere in England or Germany would be fun. We're ready to start acting like retired folks by spending next February in Florida. Pictures of the 21st Century Colbrunns can be found at www.geocities.com/djcolbrunn.

House Perspective

The very first Creative Christmas Letter that we sent almost wrote itself. I was encouraged by my husband to send a form letter but I searched my brain for a creative approach. One day, while going through a drawer of stuff that the former home-owner had left, I found a stack of stationery with an artist's rendering of our new home. It almost said to me, "I'll write your Christmas letter!" Enthralled with the idea, I sat down at our new Atari computer to write the letter from our new house. Indeed, I even personalized every letter with their family name in the greeting and a unique note in the last paragraph for each. Consequently, I had to print them one-by-one on our home printer. It was folded in thirds with the house printed upside down on the top of the back page so that it reveals the beginning of the letter when lifted. Print any continued text from the front upside down below (above) your picture/art. I used markers to add color and write a greeting. Taking more time than I wanted to devote to Christmas letters, I chose to sacrifice the personalization in future letters and only handwrite a note when needed.

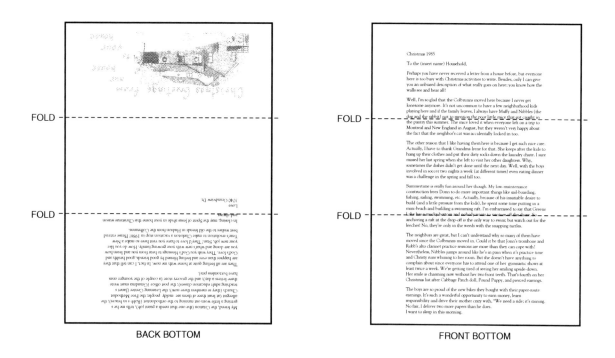

BACK BOTTOM   FRONT BOTTOM

Christmas 1985

To the *(insert name)* Household,

Perhaps you have never received a letter from a house before, but everyone here is too busy with Christmas activities to write. Besides, only I can give you an unbiased description of what really goes on here; you know how the walls see and hear all!

Well, I'm so glad that the Colbrunns moved here because I never get lonesome anymore. It's not uncommon to have a few neighborhood kids playing here and if the family leaves, I always have Muffy and Nibbles (the dog and the rabbit) not to mention the poor little mice that got caught in the pantry this summer. The mice loved it when everyone left on a trip to Montreal and New England in August, but they weren't very happy about the fact that the neighbor's cat was accidentally locked in too.

The other reason that I like having them here is because I get such nice care. Actually, I have to thank Grandma Irene for that. She keeps after the kids to hang up their clothes and put their dirty socks down the laundry chute. I sure missed her last spring when she left to visit her other daughters. Why, sometimes the dishes didn't get done until the next day. Well, with the boys involved in soccer two nights a week (at different times) even eating dinner was a challenge in the spring and fall too.

Summertime is really fun around here though. My low-maintenance construction frees Donn to do more important things like sail-boarding, fishing, sailing, swimming, etc. Actually, because of his insatiable desire to build (and a little pressure from the kids), he spent some time putting in a mini-beach and building a swimming raft. I'm embarrassed to say that Greens Lake has a mucky bottom and nobody wants to venture off the shore. So anchoring a raft at the drop-off is the only way to swim; but watch out for the leeches! No, they're only in the weeds with the snapping turtles.

The neighbors are great, but I can't understand why so many of them have moved since the Colbrunns moved in. Could it be that Jonn's trombone and Robb's alto clarinet practice sessions are more than they can cope with? Nevertheless, Nibbles jumps around like he's in pain when it's practice time and Christy runs whining to her room. But she doesn't have anything to complain about since everyone has to attend one of her gymnastic shows at least twice a week. We're getting tired of seeing her smiling upside-down. Her smile is charming now without her two front teeth. That's fourth on her Christmas list after Cabbage Patch doll, Pound Puppy, and pierced earrings.

The boys are so proud of the new bikes they bought with their paper-route earnings. It's such a wonderful opportunity to earn money, learn responsibility and drive their mother crazy with, "We need a ride; it's raining. No fair, I deliver two more papers than he does. I want to sleep in this morning."

My friend, the Citation (the one that needs a paint job), tells me he's getting a little worn out running to the orthodontist (Robb's in braces); the allergist (at least three of them are moldy people; the Free Methodist Church (they're members there now); the Learning Center (Janet's teaching adult education classes); the post office (Grandma must write three letters a day); and the grocery store (a couple of the younger ones have bottomless pits).

They are all feeling quite at home with me now. In fact, I can tell that they are happier than ever and feeling blessed by good friends, good health and God's love. They wish you God's blessings and are eager to hear from you and learn how you are doing and what's new with your growing family. How do you like your new job, Stan? They'd love to have you visit here so make a New Year's resolution to make Clarkston a vacation stop in 1986! Please extend best wishes to the old friends in Hudson from the Colbrunns.

In closing, may the Spirit of Jesus abide in your home this Christmas season and always.

Love
3740 Grandview Dr.

Family Pet's Perspective

For many of us, our pet is an important part of our family. So writing a Christmas letter from our family pet makes sense because she is always there and knows all the family secrets. The letter follows the format of a day with the family dog observing the current and past activities of each family member. Furthermore, the dog can "brag" about the family activities and make it sound like she is complaining so that the total effect is less nauseous for the reader.

STEP 1. GENERATE YOUR OWN LIST OF TOPICS TO BE INCLUDED IN YOUR LETTER.

FAMILY MEMBERS, FRIENDS OR PETS	EVENTS, TRAVELS, HUMOROUS SITUATIONS, CHANGES, ACCOMPLISHMENTS, ACTIVITIES

STEP 2. THIS THEME IS FROM THE PERSPECTIVE OF A FAMILY PET.

STEP 3. WEAVE TOPICS INTO THE THEME.
Going through a typical day, devote a paragraph to each family member's topics.

CHRISTMAS GREETINGS FROM THE COLBRUNNS

Hi! I'm Muffy, the cute one in the middle. They asked me to send this picture so you could see how the kids have grown! I'm just glad they didn't ask me to smile because I had half of my teeth removed this year.

Here I am, home alone. But that's nothing new. Would you believe that they actually left me alone for a whole weekend while they went skiing up north last February? It's a good thing that Steve, Robb's paper route buddy, came over to keep me company part of the time. They promised better treatment when they went West last summer so I stayed with friends who had a pool. The worst part of their trip was having to watch the Yellowstone slides every time we had company.

The rest of the summer was pretty exciting. Robb and Jonn saved their money to buy a jet ski. They love the power and speed. At least it keeps them off the streets. Christy made a neighborhood library out of Grandma's bedroom while she was visiting in Illinois this summer. (Don't tell Grandma!) Janet found a steady job as life-guard on the swim raft every sunny afternoon at 2:00. Jonn and Donn raced a Wayfarer sailboat with a local fleet, but seemed to do better racing the wind on a sailboard at home.

Oh good! Just when I start getting the urge to go outside, Grandma Irene comes home. She just had lunch and played bingo at the senior center. She and Lucy, her friend from down the street, went on a senior bus trip to Mackinac Island and had a wonderful time this fall. Next year it may be Hawaii!

Jonn will be home next on the high school bus but not for long. Every evening he either practices with the marching band on the trombone or teaches swim lessons at the Racquet Club. He says that it beats cleaning locker rooms there like he did last summer.

Robb will be bounding in any minute from the junior high bus. Oops, unless he has to stay after school for basketball practice or Odyssey of the Mind. His OM team took third place at the state competition last spring by building a little car, performing a skit and doing some spontaneous, problem-solving.

Well look who just got home. Janet, better known as Mom, is apt to come in at any time. She goes to aerobics on the mornings that she doesn't have classes at Oakland University. She finally decided what she wants to be when she grows up — an elementary school counselor. When she's not teaching a parenting class, or going to a committee meeting of some sort, she's chauffeuring somebody somewhere. Jonn promised to help with that job next year when he gets his drivers license and Ferrari. For some reason that makes everybody laugh.

Whoosh! Janet's gone again. It must be time for Christy's dancing lessons. She likes tap better than jazz and ballet. Maybe it's because of the gala Christmas performances her tap class participates in during the week before Christmas in Flint. She also likes being on the school newspaper staff.

I suppose Donn will be dragging in late again. Being promoted to supervisor of test operations certainly has its draw-backs, but he likes his job. Being the good dad that he is, he still found time to borrow a company truck to transport the equipment for marching band competitions. He was as proud as they when they won third place in the state. I doubt if he'll coach Robb's OM team again for the fourth year. They're a noisy group!

I'm looking forward to Christmas vacation for everyone to slow down a bit. What? Donn's family, eleven people and a dog, will be visiting for the holiday? That sounds like a lot of turkey scraps. Maybe I should get busy and write a letter to Santa for some dentures.

MUFFY

P.S. May the Christ of Christmas enter your hearts and homes during this holiday season.

Child's Perspective

The perspective for this letter is that of my 2-year-old grandson. The other theme that threads its way through this letter is "change." For us, 2001 was a year that changed our everyday life and world. A child's perspective can provide plenty of material for humor in a letter while still presenting all the details that an adult would include. We had him sitting at an antique school desk when we took the picture of him writing. The bonus he added on his own was the protruding tongue to show that he was really hard at work.

STEP 1. GENERATE YOUR OWN LIST OF TOPICS TO BE INCLUDED IN YOUR LETTER.

FAMILY MEMBERS, FRIENDS OR PETS	EVENTS, TRAVELS, HUMOROUS SITUATIONS, CHANGES, ACCOMPLISHMENTS, ACTIVITIES

STEP 2. THIS THEME IS FROM A CHILD'S PERSPECTIVE.

STEP 3. WEAVE TOPICS INTO THE THEME.

Consider your topics from a child's perspective to add humor to your letter.

Christmas Greetings.

You've probably never received a letter from a two year-old, but everyone else in the Colbrunn family is too busy to write this year. So Grandma and Grandpa (I like to call them Jana and Papa) asked me to take a break between Legos and Elmo videos to tell you about all the changes we have experienced in 2001.

Now, my Aunt Christy started us out, in this big year of change, by getting engaged on 01/01/01. That meant that we would add one more member to our family. Uncle Chris. Meanwhile Christy had to graduate with her masters degree from Regent University in community counseling in May and take a couple of extra courses for licensure in the summer, giving her six weeks left at home to prepare for their September 15th wedding. I was the ring bear bearer in the wedding which meant that I got to go down the aisle first to take the white ring bear to my daddy who was standing in the front. However, I missed out on what the guests said was quite a spiritually touching ceremony because I started to cry and had to leave. I just wanted to go see my mommy who was standing on the other side of the church but she was already holding a bunch of flowers and carrying what they said was my baby sister. But she wasn't the only one. There were two other pregnant bridesmaids not counting my Aunt Jen who had to have a stunt double in the wedding since she had her hands full (or something like that) carrying triplets. Aunt Christy said that being invited to be in her wedding was like a rite of fertility, whatever that means. There seemed to be a hassle about a lot of people not coming to the wedding because airplanes were not flying that week. So the matron of honor and her husband drove nonstop from Colorado and back but the best man didn't even have that option considering that he lives in Alaska. After a tense day of wondering if the groom could leave Andrews Air Force Base, everything else was incidental. "The groom is here!" became the response to anything else that went awry.

In addition to changing her name to Tanner, Christy also changed her address to a house they are renting in Alexandria, Virginia. She has a counseling job there with a Christian psychiatrist in private practice. Even though Uncle Chris is too busy being a doctor to come visit much, Aunt Christy managed to come back to see us on October 17 when Jonn and Jen delivered the next big change in our family: Britany Ann, Ethan Edward and Brent William. They weighed 4# 11 oz, 4# 3 oz. and 3# 13 oz. respectively. They did so well at 32 1/2 weeks that they went home within 10 days from when they were born. Now these guys are smart to come as a set. They will always have someone to play with and can take turns distracting their mom and dad to get extra cookies and things like that.

If it weren't enough to add a new uncle and three cousins, my parents, a.k.a. Robb and Joni, announced on October 27 that it was time for me to see my new baby sister. Lilia Janet has lots of long dark hair and weighed 6# 11oz. Boy, did things change around my house! She keeps my mommy and daddy very busy and the worst part is that she doesn't even like to play. At least I'll never have to worry about her playing with My toys! Mommy says that she is an easier baby and that she is glad that I was born first. I guess that means that she loves me best.

Things have changed around Jana and Papa's house too. They finished remodeling the bathroom with a fun bubble tub, just in time to work on items for Christy's wedding since she was too far away to do it all herself. That included locating a reception hall, photographer, caterer, DJ, florist and cake decorator. Even when she got home there were favors, gifts, invitations, showers, welcome baskets and programs to work on. But the big project was launched when Aunt Christy asked Papa to finish restoring the 1961 Corvette for her wedding! Uncle Jonn jumped on the bandwagon to help Papa in the race that was completed only hours before Chris and Christy drove it from the church to the reception. After writing about it in the past 13 Christmas letters, they can officially say, "The Corvette is done!" in its 40th anniversary year.

Things continued to change, even after they became official empty-nesters. Within a few weeks, they took on GRANDparenting at an intensive level. Instead of working this year as a part-time counselor, Jana is an occasional counseling coordinator so she can be a 24-#hour triplet nanny, alternating weeks with Jen's mother. When they are on "triplet duty," Papa moves in with Jonn and Jen too, and helps with the every-3-hour night feedings. The babies have doubled their weight and show no negative effects of having been born prematurely. Praise the Lord, lots of people were praying for them! Jonn and Jen gratefully accept this dramatic change in their lives, knowing they will have little relief for at least 18 years. Everyone says that caring for the triplets is exhausting and exhilarating! Regardless, I'm excited about being with them at Grandparents' Cousins Camp some day. Wait 'til they see what I can teach all these new little Colbrunns!

Being a member of the high tech generation, I didn't enclose any fuzzy pictures in this newsletter. Instead, check out the following website to see how the family has changed: http://www.geocities.com/donnjan 1960.

They say that our world changed forever on September 11. Being fairly new in this world, I hope that it has changed for the good: More love of God, more love of country and more love among people. There's only one thing that will never change and that is God's ever-present love, comfort and strength. May you celebrate that love anew this Christmas.

Merry Christmas and God Bless America.

Notes

Use this space for your own Perspective Letter theme ideas!

Consider a letter from the perspective of a…

 game show host/contestant

 book or movie reviewer

 human resource manager

 mailbox

 car

Conclusion

Because many of these themes have been painstakingly born from our imaginations, we are eager to share them and also to glean from the readers' creativity for our future letters. Hopefully, our letters will become the inspiration to create your own themes. We invite you to send your unique creative Christmas letters to us at creativechristmasletters@yahoo.com. With your permission, we will publish future editions of *Ideas For Writing Creative Christmas Letters*, which will include those authored by our readers. You can also visit our website at www.writingcreativechristmasletters.com for future ideas and for information on ordering another book.

Thank you for purchasing our book.
We enjoy bringing the spirit of Christmas to everyone!